NEUROADVANTAGE

ANDREW FULLER

NEUROADVANTAGE

The Strengths-based Approach to Neurodivergence

Published in 2025 by Amba Press, Melbourne, Australia
www.ambapress.com.au

© Andrew Fuller 2025

All rights reserved. No part of this book may be reproduced or transmitted in any form or by any means, electronic or mechanical, including photocopying, recording or by any information storage and retrieval system, without prior permission in writing from the publisher.

Cover design: Tess McCabe
Internal design: Amba Press
Editor: Andrew Campbell

ISBN: 9781923403086 Print
ISBN: 9781923403093 eBook

A catalogue record for this book is available from the National Library of Australia.

About the Author

Andrew Fuller is a clinical psychologist and family therapist who specialises in resilience, brains and learning strengths. Andrew works with schools students and parents across the world.

Andrew is an author of many books, including: *Tricky Conversations: How to Have Less Conflict and More Peace in Your Life*, *Guerrilla Tactics for Teachers: The Essential Classroom Management Guide*, *Neurodevelopmental Differentiation: Optimising Brain Systems to Maximise Learning*, *Tricky Teens and Emerging Adults: A Survival Guide for Parents*, *The A to Z of Feelings: Making Your Emotions Work For You, Not Against You!* and *Work Smarter Not Harder: Study Skills for Students Who Don't Like Homework*.

Contents

Introduction 1

Part 1 We're Going on a Treasure Hunt 7

Chapter 1   How Parenting Neurodivergent Kids Is Different 9
Chapter 2   Parenting Neurodivergent Kids from Anxious to Attached 15
Chapter 3   The Spectrum(s) 28
Chapter 4   Concentration and Attention Issues 42
Chapter 5   Sensitivities and Sensory Processing Issues 56
Chapter 6   Arguments and Defiance 66
Chapter 7   Movement and Coordination Issues or Dyspraxia 81
Chapter 8   Reading Issues or Dyslexia 95
Chapter 9   Mathematics Issues or Dyscalculia 105
Chapter 10 Drawing and Writing Issues or Dysgraphia 116
Chapter 11 Tourette's Syndrome 127
Chapter 12 Auditory Processing Issues 139

Part 2 Executive Functions 153

Chapter 13 Setting Up Your Neurodivergent Child for Success in Life 155
Chapter 14 Planning 158
Chapter 15 Concentration 160
Chapter 16 Memory 163
Chapter 17 Impulse Control 166
Chapter 18 Cognitive Flexibility 169
Chapter 19 Emotional Regulation 172
Chapter 20 Your Next Steps to Unleashing Neuroadvantage 175

Appendices 181
Author's Notes 183
Acknowledgments 187

Introduction

Imagine that you were given a job to retrofit the human species for survival. How would you do it? What sorts of people would you need?

You might look around at most people gossiping and carrying on their daily tasks and think to yourself, 'Well, if it's just left up to them, I'm not sure survival is a sure thing.'

So, what types of people do you think the human race might need?

Firstly, you could decide we need people who are good at creating systems and patterns that most people miss. We can't all spend our days just chatting and socialising.

Secondly, you might reflect that it could be helpful to have some fast-moving people who have heaps of energy, can focus on a million things at once and like excitement and fun.

Thirdly, you could consider it would be handy to have some people who are loyal, have a strong sense of justice and are prepared to stand up for what they believe in when challenged.

Then you might add in some people who can serve as an early-warning signal to the rest of us.

What today are often incorrectly labelled as 'deficits' are in fact variations of humanity that helped your ancestors and their tribes survive. Without the help of these neurodivergent people, none of us would be here.

These so-called 'disorders' and 'deficits' have never, in all of human history, been deemed so disadvantageous as to have been selected against or bred out. This will lead a wise reader like yourself to ask, 'Why not?' The answer outlined in this book is that these neurodiversities all have neuroadvantages. These are variations that should be valued rather than pathologised. They have conferred on humanity an advantage that enabled us to survive.

This is not a history book. It is a practical guide for parents and teachers who wish to discover and utilise the strengths of neurodivergent kids – to recognise and nurture the neuroadvantages of neurodiversity.

This book represents wisdom and ideas gathered not only from research but also from working with thousands of neurodiverse young people and their families. Some of them came into the clinic dragging with them a series of diagnostic categories that consumed most of the alphabet. Sometimes those diagnoses were helpful but sometimes they obscured the person the label was trying to describe. Invariably, the diagnoses did not mention the person's strengths, passions, positive attributes or human capacities. They provided a picture of troubles and deficits rather than capabilities and strengths.

Neurodivergent kids are rarely balanced

Kids are good at learning. In fact, they are faster learners than most adults. However, they often attend schools where it is implied they should try to be good at everything. This can lead some of them to conclude, 'If I am not good at everything, then I am good at nothing.'

The task facing parents and the purpose of this book is to help kids discover and value how they learn best.

Most neurodivergent kids are not all-rounders with an even spread of skills across every area. Most have some areas where they are highly competent and other areas where they really struggle. Some can eloquently express their thoughts in pictures but can hardly assemble two coherent words to describe an idea. Some will be seriously underestimated in schools that often value the fastest answer over a more hesitant but more thoughtful one. Others can talk to you in great detail and with wonderful connection but will run a mile from reading even a short paragraph.

We see this unevenness of skills because the information-processing pathways in neurodivergent brains differ. One cause of this is 'myelination'. Myelin sheathing wraps itself around different networks or circuits in the brain and speeds up thinking. About 60 per cent of the neurodivergent brain is myelinated, which of course means about 40 per cent is not.

This explains why neurodivergent kids are good at some things other people find difficult and are able to do some things other people find tricky.

The main pathways of learning strengths are shown below.

Introduction

My Learning Strengths

Planning and sequencing
Involves making a goal, organising the steps towards that goal in a logical order and either sticking with the plan or altering it if circumstances change.

Thinking and logic
Being able to problem-solve and figure things out.

Concentration and memory
Involves being focused and retaining and retrieving knowledge.

People smarts
Understanding your own emotions, the feelings of others and subtleties of social situations.

Perceptual-motor skills
Involves learning through our body and our senses.

Language and word smarts
Facility with written and spoken language. Processing language enables us to think and to remember.

Spatial reasoning
Involves thinking in pictures.

Number smarts
Thinking using numbers.

Rather than lumping a child together with others into a diagnostic group, this approach involves going on a treasure hunt to find each child's unique combination of skills, abilities and learning strengths and then working out how to use that knowledge to increase their success, confidence and happiness. Unless some of these hidden learning strengths are recognised and activated, the child may never get a chance to build success and resilience.

It doesn't matter what age a neurodivergent person is; it is never too late to strengthen the mind.

Diagnoses can be helpful for funding and some support. They can promote self-understanding but they are often limited. Most diagnostic labels focus on kids' limitations – what they can't do – and not as much on how to help them succeed. As a result, they often don't give parents (or teachers) ways to really improve outcomes for neurodivergent kids.

This approach builds on what is already strong for the child and uses that to amplify areas of learning strengths and broaden them to other areas. We start with what is strong rather than what is 'wrong'. This empowers parents to create a conversation with their child about building on their learning strengths.

This book contains many ideas that have worked to help thousands of neurodivergent kids. To get the best out of it, you will need to assess your child's learning strengths. It will take about ten minutes. To do this go to **www.mylearningstrengths.com** and complete the analysis.

You can either do this with your child or on their behalf.

A free letter will then be emailed to you outlining the top two learning strengths. A full report outlining all of the child's learning strengths, strategies to help their learning, and careers that utilise those strengths is also available for a small fee.

Occasionally, a child may disagree with the summary of their learning strengths. In these cases, either repeat the analysis with them or ask them what they believe to be their strongest areas.

Discuss the results with your child's teacher(s).

This approach helps parents, teachers and young people understand the advantages of neurodivergent brains and how to leverage and capitalise on those advantages so that we can maximise the chances for success. The analysis of learning strengths is intended as the start of a journey rather than determining the only way someone can learn.

I love working with these kids and their families. While coming up with good solutions and ways to help them access their strengths requires thinking and patience, some of the most flabbergasting, gobsmacking original ideas I have ever heard come out of the brains and mouths of our neurodivergent kids. Thank you!

How this book is structured

In Part 1, I start by talking about the big issue of helping parents function well and thrive while raising neurodivergent kids. Then I turn to an issue that afflicts every neurodivergent kid: anxiety.

Each of the following chapters then outlines a different type of neurodivergence. In each of these chapters, I:

- Identify the gifts inherent in the particular area of neurodivergence and how they can set children up for success
- Provide a brief overview of how the brains of these children differ from how other brains process learning
- Outline how parents can help
- Identify the strengths of kids with this type of neurodivergence
- Discuss the gizmos, tech and methods that help each child (I consider how the brain learns, including how it accesses, processes and retrieves information, then consider the tools available to enhance strengths and overcome barriers.)
- Summarise the parenting strategies that have a big impact, quick fixes and anything that is a waste of time.

In Part 2, I turn to the executive functions – planning, concentration, memory, impulse control, cognitive flexibility and emotional regulation – and how to develop these in children.

Part I
We're Going on a Treasure Hunt

Chapter 1

How Parenting Neurodivergent Kids Is Different

The perplexing, delightful mission of raising a neurodivergent child is an adventure that teaches all of us many lessons.

Here are 12 lessons I wish I had learned earlier.

Accept your child for who they are

This sounds simple but is often quite challenging. Your child has a unique mix of strengths, challenges and vulnerabilities. Learning and accepting these attributes of your child means that you can create for them what Maria Montessori called 'the prepared environment' – that is, the conditions and settings that will empower your child to maximise their independent learning and exploration.

Many neurodivergent kids are exquisitely sensitive to textures, lighting, sound, taste, temperature, shifts in routine, physical distance and tone of voice. Considering in what context your child feels most comfortable will make your home a haven. Your most important job is not to prepare them for the challenges of the world but to create a setting where they can grow and thrive.

Many parents go through a process of sadness, guilt and even grief about the challenges facing their child, before they can begin to accept their child for who they are. This is a tough time but is a normal process of slow acceptance.

Once you have come to terms with who your child really is, you can begin the treasure hunt to find their strengths. There truly are neuroadvantages hidden within neurodivergence.

Much of this book is designed to help you to do this.

② Accept that your child will be the expert and you will be their advocate

While there are many wonderful health and educational professionals who will be able to assist you in developing ways to help your child grow into the best version of themselves, you will always know your child best. When in doubt, you should trust your own judgment first, then, if need be, consider seeking a second opinion.

The eventual aim is for your child to be the expert of what works for them and for you to be their advocate.

③ Accept that other people will not understand

Parenting neurodivergent kids is not always a breezy walk in the park. There will be times when the excrement collides with the ventilation system. For this reason, your parenting methods may come under scrutiny by other people, especially family members.

Opinions will vary about whether you are being too soft on your child and overindulging them or being too hard and expecting too much. Just like Goldilocks, it's hard to get the mix just right in everyone's eyes.

While most of the suggestions or comments that you receive will be intended to be helpful, advice is not always helpful. Most people will base their suggestions on what has worked for their child. Their child is not *your* child. Be polite. Thank them for their input and then get on with parenting your child in ways that you know work.

④ What you do is much more powerful than what you say

The actions of neurodivergent kids (and kids in general, to be honest) are more related to the levels of neurochemicals in their brains than their thoughts about events. This means that what you do is much more powerful than what you say. We'll expand on this in the next chapter.

5 If we don't sleep, we don't function

A sleep-deprived neurodivergent kid is a bad day about to happen. Throw in a sleep-deprived parent, and we have double trouble.

You will need to plan your family's sleep routine with the clarity of a determined general.

Firstly, think about how much quality sleep you need to function well as a parent. How many hours? Is it one long sleep or two shorter ones? Do naps play a role?

Then, how much sleep does your child need to be at their best?

How much wind-down time does your child need to get ready to sleep?

What is the best evening wind-down process for your family?

Once you have determined the parameters, you need to work out a family routine that you put into place almost every day to achieve the amount of sleep everyone needs.

This is not an area of life with neurodivergent kids where you can just see how things unfold every day. As sporting coaches say, purposeful planning creates peak performance.

6 Routines for managing the rush hours

The times of the day that create the most distress for parents are the morning and evening rush hours of getting up and ready in time and getting to bed on time. Think about the different stages or accomplishments you would like to see in your home. Visually display these as a poster, and colour-code each step.

For example:

Step 1: stop playing games and start moving towards sleep

Step 2: brush teeth

Step 3: toilet then bath or shower time

Step 4: get pyjamas on

Step 5: bedtime story

Step 6: lights out

Sleep: pheew!

You may even want to create a coloured checklist of these to signal to your child which stage is next (which is often more powerful that verbal reminders).

Build the habit of a successful routine slowly, step by step, until you are creating your rush hour routine without too many hiccups. You want your child to be in such a routine that they know, 'This is just the way we do things here.'

As they develop, you will want to slowly move them towards more independence, one step at a time. You might start helping them to independently put their pyjamas on. Aim to do this for about six weeks before moving on to another independent step, such as brushing teeth.

This is known as 'backward chaining', where over time we lessen the amount of involvement parents have in each step, starting with the last step in the sequence and working back towards the first step.

Managing boilovers and meltdowns

Boilovers

These are heated disputes that become emotional to the point where there needs to be a lull in discussions before solutions can be found. Give yourself space to regain your calm. Have a cool-down phase. Try to learn what helps the child to cool down. It could be being left alone, listening to music, playing a computer game, or sometimes even getting a hug and a reassuring word. Keep them safe and help them calm.

Meltdowns

This is where the fight-or-flight part of a child's brain called the amygdala hijacks the rest of the brain. Once the internal security system has kicked in, there is no point trying to press for a solution. They will act wildly, say the most horrendous things and behave erratically.

If you continue to intervene, they will go berserk on you. The child's levels of the stress hormones adrenaline and cortisol have soared and, until they have settled again, negotiating with them will place you in a very precarious position.

In a fair and reasonable world, children would suddenly have a blinding flash of enlightenment, see the errors of their ways and start behaving in more sociable, polite and respectful ways. The chances of this happening are zilch, nada, zero, not happening any time soon. No, if change is to occur, you are going to have to be the one to kick it off.

What do I want to see start happening?

What is one thing I am doing that I should stop doing?

What is one thing I am not doing that I should start doing?

What is one thing I am doing that I should do more often?

What is the first sign that things are improving?

Co-regulation

Most neurodivergent kids can't calm by themselves. They need your help to do this. Essentially there are two main pathways in the brain. The first is activated by the amygdala and causes stress, fear and argumentativeness. The other pathway is triggered when the pituitary gland and the hypothalamus secrete the hormones oxytocin and vasopressin. These are the hormones of trust, connection and belonging. We'll discuss how parents and teachers can activate this second pathway in the next chapter.

8 Give yourself the gift of time (and forgiveness)

Raising a neurodivergent child is a journey that takes years. Along the way it will require many tweaks and refinements. Essentially it is a treasure hunt to uncover and build on your child's gifts and learning strengths. Doing this will have its twists and turns, its successes as well as some changes of course. The payoff from this treasure hunt is to curate for your child a life of as much independence, empowerment and success as you can.

9 Childhood can't be rushed

We live in a world that often seems to treat childhood as an ailment to be remedied or rushed along. The reality of parenting neurodivergent kids should free you from this madness. In a world of accelerating returns, erratically quick changes and a strange competitive race of whose child jumps through specific developmental hoops at the youngest age (as if that ever predicted anything!), you can stand aside. Be completely confident that your child will develop at their own individual rate.

10. How screens can be a useful ally

You may struggle to agree with this! The world is often focused on ineffectually trying to limit the amount of screen time young people have.

The truth is that for your neurodivergent child, screens are essential. For many, screens will dominate their working lives. For quite a few, a large proportion of their social lives will be conducted online. Most of the devices that can assist them to overcome what were once insurmountable barriers to their learning, communication and success have screens.

This does not mean that screens should take over their lives. You will need to preserve and defend family routines and rituals around bedtimes, exercise, play times and device-free mealtimes. You will need to hold these firmly.

Once those rituals and routines are in place, I recommend becoming as tech savvy as you possibly can be to advantage your child in as many ways as you can. Look forward to a life where you not only know about the latest games, gizmos and tech-wizardry, but you also use them and play them with your child.

11. Nature is your best friend

I know this is not always possible, but getting your child outdoors and into nature is one of the most powerful and therapeutic manoeuvres a parent can undertake.

12. Be kind to yourself

Parenting any child is a wonderful, time-consuming, fulfilling, exhausting, enchanting, infuriating quest. Parenting a neurodivergent child is all that plus some. Not only will there be bewildering times when you scratch your head and wonder what is next, but you will also have other adults providing you with unsolicited 'helpful' advice.

Your child is not the perfect child, and it is highly likely that you are not the perfect parent. Accept it. Love yourself and them anyway. Forgive yourself when you make mistakes.

Chapter 2

Parenting Neurodivergent Kids from Anxious to Attached

Being neurodivergent is hard work.

Every neurodivergent child is afflicted with anxiety. Feelings of being different, working hard to decipher social signals, constantly trying to hide behaviours that others might see as 'weird', not to mention wondering whether the rest of society actually consider themselves 'normal' or should be considered for serious psychotropic medication – it's all stressful and exhausting.

Trying to settle some of these kids is a bit like trying to calm a slippery, wriggling salmon. Parents of neurodivergent kids need to have really good strategies for helping their children out of anxiety and moving towards activation, approach and attach.

Behind the behaviour of most children and teens is the lower part of their brains that processes fear and anxiety. What drives that lower part of their brains are neurochemicals.

Understanding how to change the levels of neurochemicals gives parents and teachers a greater range of ways of influencing neurodivergent kids' behaviours and wellbeing.

Artwork by Ray Eckermann.

Attach ← Approach ← Activate ← Agitate ← Avoid ← Attack

Attack

The behaviours associated with this include anger, argumentativeness and attacks directed towards others or towards the self, including anxiety, fear and being overly reactive to small events.

The state of wariness and watchfulness that cortisol induces is really good for situations where there is something that wants to either eat you or kill you, but as a way of living your life it sucks.

Anyone who has tried to rationalise with an anxious child ('Maybe it is not as big an issue as you fear it could be') knows how futile reassurances can be.

The golden rule for anxiety is that it is a signal that we need to do something differently. Anxiety only really becomes a problem when we don't do anything with it. Until we physically act, fears linger and loom larger.

The quickest way to calm the mind is to exert the body.

Some strategies:

- Always speak in a calm voice with unconditional positive regard.
- Offer them something to eat or drink (drinking water reduces cortisol).

- Use more visuals and fewer words:
  - Movement
  - Walking
  - Listening
  - Safety
  - Soothing
  - Exercise.
- Identify triggers and talk about this with the child when developing a focus plan.
- Give kids space, and if they need to move, let them!

Avoid

This is the belief that if we run away from things and bury our heads in the sand and opt out, all our problems will magically vanish. Dream on!

Any parent or teacher who has provided an encouraging pep talk ('You can do it!') has already tasted true failure. The ability of neurodivergent kids to dig their heels in and not do something they feel anxious about leaves you in no doubt about their determination.

Avoidance is mainly driven by the neurochemical adrenaline.

Many young people only have so much 'Get up and go' to give. Adrenaline energises us when used well. We need to gradually increase the number of challenges our young people take on. Interspersing fast thinking with slow thinking is one way. This is a measured mix of brief challenges or tasks followed by recovery times.

Some strategies:

- Feed them.
- Validate how the young person is feeling ('I can see that you're frustrated') and offer two choices ('Would you like to do … or …?').
- Alter the pattern: take a break to re-focus, encourage movement, play a drama game: charades or celebrity heads.
- Return to passion and learning strengths areas.
- Have calm conversations.
- Encourage little starts with low or no stakes.
- Mention strengths but don't push them!

Agitate

The neurochemicals cortisol and adrenaline predispose people towards vigilance when threats are amplified, and creativity and playfulness are squashed. This is the last thing we want for our children.

Over time we want to settle and calm agitated brains. Talk to kids about stress and get them to identify where they can feel it in their body. Build their capacity to be self-aware.

The antidote to agitation is a sense of certainty and a sense of control. Knowing that your actions make a difference, that you can improve on your current situation, and that others are there to help you lessens fear and wariness.

Some strategies:

- Give children choices and options.
- Give them autonomy.
- Ask children to do what they are currently doing.
- Give kids space and if they need to move, ask them to go outside.
- Provide sensory items: kinetic sand, soft bean bags, aromas they like, or anything soft to touch.
- Switch from fast thinking to slow thinking ('Think of five animals as quick as you can – now tell me which one is your favourite and why').

Activate

Dopamine is the neurochemical that creates motivation. It is derived from the amino acid tyrosine.

Not only does dopamine energise us and move us into action, but it also improves learning and memory. Challenges, problem-solving, quizzes, puzzles, socialising and rhythmic movements such as drumming are all ways to increase dopamine.

Some strategies:

- Positive feedback
- Enjoyable challenges
- Guessing games that are fun
- Getting enough sleep
- Being listened to
- Rhythmic movements
- Patterned repetitive activities: table tennis, basketball, handball, dancing, volleyball, ping pong, juggling, drumming, down ball

- Quizzes, puzzles
- Exercise
- Being in nature
- Fun.

Approach

The most powerful anti-depressant known to humankind is produced free of charge, prescription-free, in your body and brain: serotonin. It is derived from the amino acid tryptophan.

Increased levels of serotonin are associated with feelings of happiness, contentment and wellbeing. We all benefit from being in the company of people whom we like and trust and who recognise our strengths and contributions. In families and schools we can create cultures of appreciation where everyone is acknowledged as having different strengths and contributions (and feel happier).

Some strategies:

- Kindness
- Acknowledgment
- Play
- Humour
- Asking questions they know the answer to.

Attach

Recent times have created a lessening of trust in the world. Feelings of certainty – knowing who to rely on and who our true allies are – have all been thrown into question.

We need to restore a sense of trust and integrity in our families and schools where these values have been shaken up.

Oxytocin and vasopressin are the hormones that underpin our sense of attachment to trustworthy others. Securing a sense of attachment sets people on a trajectory towards creating quality relationships.

Some strategies:

- Create positive routines and rituals that promote belonging and safety.
- Be reliable and trustworthy – follow through.
- Be kind.
- Tell your kids that you love them and keep reminding them.

- Give them hugs.
- Give them special treats.
- Play games with them.
- Spend time with them.
- Increase caring and consistency.
- Give them space to explore and a safe base to always come back to.
- Value them for who they are rather than what they can do.
- Don't give too much space to fear talk.
- Believe in them.
- Support their dreams.

Anxiety and neurodivergence

When anxiety affects fairly neurotypical kids, some become 'chatty and scatty' while others become 'broody and moody'. Applying neurotypical interventions to neurodivergent kids rarely works. We need to be more tailored in our approaches. About 30 per cent of school students are neurodivergent.

Unfortunately, neurodivergent kids are much more susceptible to being afflicted by anxiety, and when they are, they have distinctive needs in order to calm down and process their thinking and learning.

While neurodivergent kids are often incredibly fearless and courageous in dealing with life, their big area of vulnerability is anxiety. It can take over their lives. Neurodivergent kids often feel overwhelmed and paralysed by anxiety. They can spend long periods of time huddled away trying desperately to avoid situations that provoke their anxious feelings. Left unmanaged, anxiety can severely limit what they can do in their lives.

Unmanaged anxiety hits our body even more powerfully than our minds. It suppresses our immune system, disrupts our sleep patterns, depletes our energy levels, and narrows our loves to a few 'safe' activities. Anxiety also causes changes in learning and information processing in our brains.

Top-down and bottom-up approaches

Shifting behaviour involves two processes. One is **bottom-up** and is driven mainly by the levels of neurochemicals in our brains. The second

Neuroadvantages of kids with anxiety

Planning and sequencing
- ✓ Learning to plan; try out the plan, then alter the plan if need be

Thinking and logic
- ✓ Scenario-building
- ✓ Predictions
- ✓ Probabilities

People smarts
- ✓ May prefer a few close and trusted friends
- ✓ Tuned into others' feelings

Concentration and memory
- ✓ Good focus on threats, less on feelings of safety

Anxiety

Language and word smarts
- ✓ Poetry
- ✓ Songwriting
- ✓ Blogging
- ✓ Posting on social media

Perceptual-motor skills
- ✓ Calming the mind through physical activity

Spatial reasoning
- ✓ Doodling
- ✓ Modelling clay
- ✓ Art

Number smarts
- ✓ Some fear numbers; for others the certainty of numbers is a relief

© Andrew Fuller, *Neuroadvantage: The Strengths-based Approach to Neurodivergence* (Amba Press, 2025)

is **top-down** and is driven by mindsets, attitudes and the key skills that predict academic success in schools. These skills can be implemented and developed at any age. However, if the **bottom-up** process is 'out of sorts', there is very little chance for the top-down process to work effectively.

There are clear strategies that can be used by every family and in any classroom to help young people to shift from attack to attach. While top-down strategies often include kind words that help change thinking, bottom-up strategies more often involve doing things together.

As babies, we all firstly learned to calm ourselves by being calmed. This involved being held, rocked, sung to, soothed and loved. When we are stressed and fearful, it is those most basic but also most essential non-verbal actions that we turn to. These are the kind gestures and actions that build oxytocin and vasopressin and trust.

How parents can help

Generally speaking, anxiety is a signal, a 'call to do something'. It mobilises us and lets us know that something in our world is scary and requires changing. Anxiety only really becomes a problem for most of us when we don't use that signal to do something about it.

Remember, the quickest way to relax the mind is to exert the body.

Step 1: Find their learning strengths

Parents can complete the analysis of learning strengths at www.mylearningstrengths.com, either with their child or on their behalf, and use the free letter to start a conversation about building on their identified strengths. Discuss these with your child's teacher(s). A full report is also available outlining strategies, strengths and possible future career areas.

Learning strengths can help neurodivergent kids to understand that they have some areas where they perform well but also have some areas that are more challenging. This is helpful in many areas of their lives and is especially useful in helping them manage their anxieties about assessments at schools.

Many neurodivergent young people feel terrified and panic in tests and exams or freeze when called on in class. This can make some avoidant of school. Others incorrectly assume that they are not clever and cannot be successful. Another group decide that if they can't be successful academically, they will pursue social success as the class clown or the cutest, most vulnerable kid in class.

This can cause some adults to respond by trying to be kind but inadvertently treating the child as less capable than they truly are.

Step 2: Build on their learning strengths

Helping these kids (and their teachers) to identify and build on their learning strengths increases self-belief and feelings that they can succeed.

Let's look at some of the main learning strengths in terms of learning and calming.

Spatial reasoning

Thinking in pictures and symbols is a learning strength that is especially worthy of development in kids who suffer from anxiety.

Stress particularly inhibits our production of language and words. If you have ever been 'shocked speechless', you may know this.

Being able to communicate information visually rather than verbally helps anxious kids to experience success.

These kids will also recover from anxiety more quickly when they use their learning strengths. When we focus on what we are good at, we calm. Colouring in, mapping, drawing, doodling, designing and even body mapping their feelings will help calm them.

Perceptual-motor skills

These kids absorb knowledge powerfully when they learn it physically or sensorily. These are sensitive kids who are attuned to their sensory inputs. Help them to notice pleasant as well as fearful feelings.

Performance anxiety and embarrassment can stifle the development of this learning strength. Help these kids to develop and practise skills away from the gaze and judgment of peers.

Help neurodivergent kids to calm their anxiety by learning interoception or how to attend to and interpret the signals from one's body. Many find repetition, ritual and specified calming places in school and at home helpful. Others find that weighted blankets or deep pressure on their body helps.

Some will seek out sensations in order to calm, others will avoid sensation and need time alone, and yet others will become overstimulated and distract others. Finding what textures, colours, aromas or movements are calming for a neurodivergent kid helps.

We all use calming movements to settle ourselves. You may have seen someone who is feeling stressed rubbing the back of their neck or behind their ears and then sighing deeply in order to calm themselves. Teenagers often yawn to achieve this.

Some neurodivergent kids do this in more noticeable ways such as large gestures or flapping their hands. This is sometimes called 'stimming'. These are important calming methods for them and should not be discouraged.

Concentration and memory

It is hard to focus in school when you feel terrified or preoccupied by what others may think of you. Anxiety, left unchecked, plays havoc with learning strengths in concentration and memory.

Helping 'chatty and scatty' kids pick out the most important aspects of a topic is a learning strength worth developing. 'Moody and broody' kids can be helped to develop the skills of note-taking. Both groups can develop their memory to high levels.

Getting them to splash their face with cold water or place their hands in a basin of warm water helps some kids. Sound reduction though noise-cancelling earbuds or headphones can help focus. Other kids find their concentration is best after doing 'heavy work' such as pulling, pushing or lifting some weights and using their large muscles.

Planning and sequencing

Many anxious kids fail tests before they even take them. They over-plan and anticipate every possible difficulty. Disasters loom large. Fears of failure hound them.

Uncertainty and ambiguity amplify anxiety. Help them to plan systematic, realistic steps towards success. Goals can heighten anxiety for these kids; systems and rituals calm them.

Help them not to get ahead of themselves. Anticipatory thinking often predicts humiliation and feeds a sense of dread. Catch them when they are mentally focusing on the future and gently direct them back to the present and to the plans they have made. Ask, 'What is the next step to do?'

Developing a learning strength in planning and sequencing helps anxious kids to base their actions on logical steps that relate to desired outcomes rather than on their current feelings and preoccupations.

Neurodivergent kids may need to start by locating where in their own body they feel worried or strong and focused. Progressive relaxation can appeal to these kids.

Planning is the art of prediction. Help them to plan for good outcomes, not just bad ones.

If events become overwhelming, it is always good to have an escape plan, ideally to a chill-out spot or a person they trust.

Thinking and logic

Most neurodivergent kids can think things through. However, some develop 'sticky' brains where they get stuck on their thoughts.

Helping anxious kids learn the scientific method advantages them greatly. Simply put, this is:

1. Gather together data (what you know).
2. Form a best idea (a hypothesis).
3. Test out your idea. This may include evaluating threats or opportunities.
4. Ask, 'Is the hypothesis still the best idea?'
5. Make a conclusion.

This stills the endless treadmill of repetitive thinking and overcomes the tendency to base their thinking entirely on their feelings.

Distraction, chess, Rubik's cubes, mindfulness, puzzles, trail-making and activities like joining the dots or walking a labyrinth can calm these kids.

People smarts

These kids are so tuned into other people that they almost never calm by themselves. They require interactions with someone they trust to calm.

Anxious kids often fear negative evaluations by others. This makes it hard for them to utilise feedback and make changes.

Developing learning strengths in people smarts contributes greatly to the success of neurodivergent kids. As some view the world as potentially hostile, working out who can be trusted is a process of reading others well.

It is also important to learn that feelings of anxiety are signals but are not always accurate, and over time to build an inner confidence that is not reliant on other people.

Singing, humming, chanting, becoming a 'feeling detective', matching someone else's movements and breathing patterns can help. Patting a pet and walking and talking are invaluable.

Language and word smarts

At times, we are all quite good at creating disaster scenarios that can feature in our own imaginary, personal horror show. Neurodivergent kids are often especially adept at imagining the worst possible outcomes.

Anxiety can leave even the most articulate of us stumbling and mumbling. Helping neurodivergent kids to express their ideas and feelings through drawing, poetry, songs, writing, music, video or dance will help build this area.

Performance anxiety, including fear of speaking in public, inhibits the development of this learning strength. We can begin overcoming this in childhood by providing opportunities to be involved in performances in practical non-speaking roles and gradually increasing their level of participation and verbal contributions.

Stories, fear-busting methods, reading and developing conversational skills are all helpful. We want to create supportive spaces where neurodivergent kids feel their voice is heard and valued.

Number smarts

Generally, this is the learning strength with the largest barrier for anxious kids. Around 17 per cent of people suffer high levels of mathematics anxiety.

Quite a few neurodivergent kids, however, find the solidity of numbers to be comforting. The clarity of numbers is free of ambiguity. It's almost as if, when some of them think in numbers, they don't need to deal with all that confusing 'feeling stuff'.

Use rating scales such as asking, 'On a scale of one to ten, where ten is the worst, where are you right now?'

Using numbers to help neurodivergent kids focus on the range of their feelings can be useful. For example, see if they can notice:

*6 things you can **see***

*5 things you can **hear***

*4 things you can **smell***

*3 things you can **touch***

*2 things you can **taste***

*1 **feeling** you have (other than anxiety)*

Leveraging their strengths with gizmos, tech and methods

I have found the following apps useful:

- **Brainwaves.** This app will get a mention many times in this book. I use it a lot. It requires using earbuds or headphones and provides the listener with 35 different programs that alter their brainwave patterns. Our favourite settings are 'powernap' and 'deep rest'.
- **Headspace for Kids.** This is a mindfulness app offering guided meditation and relaxation exercises tailored for children, helping them manage stress and sensory overload. It includes meditation sessions specifically designed for focus, relaxation and sleep.
- **Mental Stillness.** Produced by our great colleagues at Generation Next, this free app is well researched and effective.

Chapter 3

The Spectrum(s)

We often speak of 'the spectrum', but most young people vary on many different dimensions. For this reason, I prefer to talk about 'the spectrums'.

One of the gifts of being somewhere on the spectrums is an awareness of patterns and systems.

Many neurotypical people spend considerable amounts of their lives fearing what other people might think of them and puzzling about social issues that never eventuate. People on the autism spectrums may have some immunity to these afflictions.

The gift of being somewhere on the spectrums sets kids up for a life of deep authenticity, loyalty and integrity. Within the areas of interest they develop, there is deep, serious passion and an intense knowledge of details.

In the long term these gifts set people up for success in careers in technology, commerce, coding, science, engineering, business and manufacturing.

Whatever category or description we might apply to a neurodivergent person, we want to value the diversity of their strengths and their unique individuality.

Young people on the spectrums vary greatly in their abilities and learning strengths. Each person is different. However, it can be helpful to think about these variations along several main dimensions or spectrums. Considering different dimensions or spectrums helps us to understand each child better as an individual.

Some of the main spectrums are:

Systematic thinking	Empathic thinking
Focuses in on a few thoughts	Links different ideas and thoughts
Interested in 'things'	Interested in people
Desire for routine	Likes change and spontaneity
Narrow range of interests	Broader range of interests
Effectively communicates	Ineffectively communicates

Each person is different. Neurodivergent kids are different in different ways. It takes them some time to learn how to care for themselves best, and it takes teachers and parents time to understand how to bring out the best in them.

Mapping where people are on the above six spectrums gives us a richer basis for planning how to maximise their success.

Discovering the neuroadvantages in the spectrums

Kids who are on these spectrums possess attributes and strengths that others do not have. They also face some challenges ahead in their lives.

It is often easier to think about the challenges and overlook the strengths that give these kids advantages. Success in life is more often about capitalising on what you do well rather than improving on what you don't do well.

Many of them have a fine eye for detail and notice small shifts in patterns that other people would overlook. Many of them are skilled at using their spatial and visual reasoning and can often organise visual information into patterns.

Generally, they are discerning people with high interest in a few key areas and almost zero interest in other areas. With their passions, their interests and their strengths, they have incredibly detailed memory and an almost encyclopedic level of knowledge. Shift over to an area that does not spark their interest, and their eyes glaze over, they start to yawn and they look really bored.

Kids on the spectrums often score higher on non-verbal parts of IQ tests and are often suited to careers as programmers, systems analysts, engineers, mechanics or scientists.

The brains of neurodivergent kids are different, but it is important to always remember that difference does not equal deficit.

Young brains with autism or on the spectrums (non-neuro-nerds look away now!) commonly manifest:

- Higher levels of serotonin than most other people, which means they are usually quite happy-go-lucky (except when something ruffles their routines and then they can become distressed or grumpy).
- There is some debate in the research literature about this, but the mirror neurons that enable most of us to learn by watching and imitating other people appear not to work in quite the same way. They learn in their own ways and on their own terms.
- The lowered reliance on imitating others means that the social world of others can be totally bewildering. Sometimes the puzzle of other people just seems like too much hard work. On the occasions when they do decide to try to fit in, they may need to have particular social norms and expectations explained clearly.
- The areas that most people use to think about social situations may function differently. In particular, the medial prefrontal cortex and the temporoparietal junction are involved in the ability to understand that other people have different thoughts or may see things differently to ourselves. This is known as 'theory of mind'.
- Often they will have some delay in language or reading.
- The lower part of their brain, the cerebellum, which helps to coordinate smooth movements, develops more slowly, meaning that some of these kids can be uncoordinated.

Their areas of strength in terms of brain functioning include:

- being good systematisers, pattern-makers and organisers
- being good at learning and following rules
- having good musical pitch
- having a good memory.

Neuroadvantages of kids on the spectrums

Planning and sequencing
- ✓ Visual planning
- ✓ Predictability
- ✓ Advance notice of changes

Thinking and logic
- ✓ Literal thinking
- ✓ Categorisation
- ✓ Knowledge in specific interest areas
- ✓ Logical reasoning

People smarts
- ✓ Can learn the 'rules' of social engagement
- ✓ Props as conversation starters

Concentration and memory
- ✓ Routines plus some novelty
- ✓ Schedules
- ✓ Colour coding

Language and word smarts
- ✓ Learning from audio recordings
- ✓ Pairing pictures and words
- ✓ Learning from YouTube clips
- ✓ Speech-to-text apps
- ✓ Word-prediction skills

Perceptual-motor skills
- ✓ Calming through textures and aromas

Spatial reasoning
- ✓ Pattern recognition
- ✓ Checklists
- ✓ Linking feelings and colours

Number smarts
- ✓ Numerical reasoning
- ✓ Structured outlines
- ✓ Routines
- ✓ Formulas
- ✓ Systematic approaches
- ✓ Hands-on experiential mathematics

© Andrew Fuller, *Neuroadvantage: The Strengths-based Approach to Neurodivergence* (Amba Press, 2025)

How parents can help

While this book will suggest lots of strategies, let's be really clear: the most important aim of any parent is to have as wonderful a relationship with their child as they possibly can. This is more important than school and more important than any strategy. So, if you try something and it just doesn't work with your kid, never, ever let it damage your relationship. Drop it, move on and try something else.

Parenting methods that can work with neurotypical kids usually don't work with young people on the spectrums.

Let's convert that into a headline message:

Parenting methods that work with neurotypical kids usually don't work with neurodivergent young people!!!

Kids on the spectrums may find their anxiety heightened at times when they have to shift from one thing to another (for example, getting out of the house and going to school, changes in classes or routines, and having different teachers). As far as possible, give them a heads-up on changes in routine in advance.

While many of these transition points are regular events that we can prepare them for, there are always events that occur 'out of the blue'. When unexpected shifts in routines occur, we need to help them to learn what to do when they don't know what to do.

Having a Plan B or a fallback strategy – such as asking for a specific teacher or calling a parent – can save a lot of angst for everyone.

As you will see later in this chapter, several new gizmos and methods exist that help these kids to overcome challenges and to be successful.

Velcro and slippery thoughts

For kids on the spectrums, some thoughts fail to stick and slip away from their awareness as if they are highly slippery. It takes many kids 24 repetitions to get to about an 80 per cent recall of some ideas. For your neurodivergent kid, it could be more. Be prepared to calmly remind them. The fine art, of course, is how to do this without being seen as nagging. Visual charts of key activities are better and may also save your voice.

Other thoughts are so sticky that they become glued or Velcroed onto their consciousness. Generally, those ideas then go on a high-rotation inner playlist. Trying to verbally shift a Velcro thought often results in a conversation that goes on and on. Try instead changing the context – shifting rooms, going for a walk, or changing postures, such as sitting down if you've started by standing, or vice versa.

How to build your child's strengths so they are less likely to have these issues

Many kids on the spectrums have command avoidance, which means the 'Do as I say' approach that may work with some neurotypical kids never works with them. This is why parents of neurodivergent kids should cheerfully thank other people who want to provide parents 'advice' based on what worked for their neurotypical kids and then, just as cheerfully, quietly ignore whatever they have suggested.

Trying to force one of these kids to do something they really don't want to do is not only futile, it's exhausting. Applying rewards and enforcing consequences does not work.

Special interests are one of the great joys of these kids. Identifying these passions and learning strengths and building on them increases their confidence and success. Usually, these kids do not have a wide range of interests, preferring to develop strengths in a narrow range of areas.

Step 1: Find their learning strengths

Complete the analysis of learning strengths at www.mylearningstrengths.com.

If you want to, do this firstly for yourself.

You will receive an email outlining your two strongest learning strengths.

Then you may complete their analysis with or on behalf of your child.

Again, you will receive an email from me outlining your child's two strongest learning strengths.

Step 2: Build on their learning strengths

We create success for our children when we start from what is strong.

Use your child's top two learning strengths and combine this knowledge with the information below to start building their neuroadvantage.

Spatial reasoning

Kids on the spectrums are often strong in the area of visual and spatial learning. While they may not interpret emotions on faces very accurately, they are often interested in visual displays and are able to see how different parts of a picture or a machine interconnect (spatial reasoning).

Presenting daily learning and household routines visually is often a successful approach. Visual planners that show different activities throughout the day can assist in shifting from one activity to another.

Using visual timers that show how long it is before something happens can be useful. Visual checklists are handy for common tasks that need to be completed.

First–Then charts and diagrams can also be helpful:

Associating different feelings – hungry, angry, tired, lonely, stressed – with different colours helps children to identify and express their feelings.

Perceptual-motor skills

This is the use of the body and the senses in learning. Start by helping your child to learn to look where you are pointing. Using physical cues to direct attention not only increases concentration but also helps your child start to 'read' the intentions of others.

Many kids on the spectrums are adept at using their perceptions and motor skills in learning. As I have noted, some will have set physical routines known as stimming for calming themselves when they are upset. It is best to accept their use of these methods.

Knowing the sensory sensitivities of these kids not only calms them but can also help their learning.

Many of these kids bond and connect with other people by doing things with them rather than just talking with them. Walking together, dancing, and playing fun games that mirror the other person's movements or facial expressions are great activities.

Encourage activities that build this learning strengths area: yoga, stretching, swimming or simple obstacle courses.

In school, seats that allow them to move, such as wobble chairs, can help.

Some kids with learning strengths in perceptual-motor skills learn physical routines really well and some enjoy quite arduous 'heavy work' that exercises their large muscle groups.

Concentration and memory

In 2004 the average concentration span was two and a half minutes; today it is forty-seven seconds. It would be almost impossible to do this research on neurodivergent kids, because their focus varies so much under different circumstances.

This is where it gets tricky: neurodivergent kids on the spectrums need consistency, but they also need stimulation to concentrate. The aim is a state of relaxed stimulation.

The sensitivity of kids on the spectrums means they often have great memories for specific areas of information and a complete lack of interest in others. Concentration can be increased by relating discussion to key interest areas, or using noise-cancelling headphones or earbuds.

No one has unlimited concentration or memory, so it is always helpful to know the main things we need to focus on and for how long.

Advance knowledge helps. For example: 'This is the work we are going to do first, then we are going to do …' It is useful to have the kids repeat back or paraphrase directions.

We need strategies to initiate and sustain concentration, such as:

- checklists for task/routine completion
- extra time on tests and assignments
- exercise and movement breaks
- reminders to keep track of time and to remind them to shift to different activities or tasks.

Planning and sequencing

Kids with learning strengths in this area love routines and predictability. This means they are able to deepen their learning and develop skills.

We can increase the predictability of plans through printed schedules or checklists using both words and pictures. We can develop thinking routines such as finding the main idea, looking at how ideas link together, and differentiating ideas that are similar from those that are different.

Using images and photographs, we can create storyboards of regular routines and possible variations.

These kids are often better at routines than flexibility. One way to increase flexibility is to map an issue out like a decision-tree with the options 'yes', 'no' and 'roadblock'. When we reach a roadblock, we need to plan differently.

It is helpful to do advance planning around unexpected changes in routines and likely problems. This empowers kids to work out possible solutions rather than panicking. When life throws a curve ball into our plans, it can be useful to have a menu of coping strategies, often depicted visually.

Some of these kids are great at planning but find it hard to get started. Take a load off these kids' minds by suggesting options: 'Would you like to do ... first or ... first?' If they refuse those, add another option and repeat: 'So would you like to do ... [new option] or ... or ... first?' Let them make decisions.

Thinking and logic

The intricacy of thinking of kids with this learning strength can be phenomenal. Kids on the spectrums are often deep thinkers and good problem-solvers. In their areas of interest, their capacity to think profoundly about issues and come up with creatively logical solutions can be jaw-dropping.

Some are literal thinkers who learn best when we provide concrete real-world examples. For example, time as an abstract concept is more easily understood when we start from time elapsed on a clock or a yearly diary or a calendar. Using paper diaries and notebooks may be better than using digital versions. Going shopping and buying items teaches kids about money.

Sorting, grouping and categorising different types of concepts can deepen children's thinking. For example: 'Dolphins, antelopes and kangaroos are all types of …'

Others are more ruminative thinkers. They almost wear out their ideas with overuse. Help them to embellish their ideas by developing thinking chains. For example, the first idea leads to the second idea …

Some get stuck when we need to choose to follow different thinking pathways. Develop decision-making trees and algorithms. Visually map ideas using logic and show how conclusions can lead us to crossroads where we can follow branch roads.

> *Jane thinks Ali is good at drawing. Is Ali good at drawing? (maybe)*
>
> *Should I ask Ali to paint my portrait? (maybe)*
>
> *That is a safe road to cross, but it's very dangerous at rush hour. Will it be safe tomorrow? (depends on what time)*
>
> *Should I cross the road at 5pm? (no)*
>
> *Should I cross at the traffic lights at 5pm? (yes)*
>
> *The sign says it is safe for experienced swimmers only.*
>
> *Does that mean if you swim a long way out you will be safe? (not necessarily)*

People smarts

Even if these kids are not especially tuned in to people, developing this learning strength as much as they can will have benefits.

Friendship skills can be strengthened through understanding taking turns and reciprocal communication.

Some kids on the spectrums master the art of masking and, in an attempt to fit in, can go along with whatever their friends might be doing. While this is usually good, there are times when it all becomes exhausting and goes pear-shaped.

The world of social interactions can be perplexing and anxiety-provoking for some. Developing acting and drama skills can be a way of rehearsing social situations, trying out different social behaviours and increasing their repertoire of responses.

Practising greetings, asking questions and guessing how other people might be feeling are all helpful skills to strengthen. Using videos and playing guessing games – such as 'What feeling is that person having?' – are not only fun but can eventually set your child up to live independently.

Start by building up their knowledge of their own feelings. This is done by saying, 'I think you might be feeling (insert name of feeling) at the moment?'

Learning 'people reading' and conversational skills is a major long-term advantage. Find pictures of people showing different feelings on their faces and play a game of 'Guess the feeling'.

Having a prop such as a book that can be used to start a conversation makes it easier for many kids.

Language and word smarts

Kids on the spectrums with strengths in language and words can create eloquent and expressive stories.

Pairing pictures, images and other visuals with reading passages often increases comprehension. Some will find it difficult to get started in creative writing, so a series of story and sentence starters can be handy. Having a word bank of vocabulary terms that can be used in writing assignments is useful as it lowers anxiety and procrastination.

Outlines of story and essay formats and structures can help to build this strength, as can checklists for editing and graphic organisers.

A number of apps are available to assist neurodivergent kids in this area, including:

- audiobooks and podcasts
- speech-to-text software
- word-prediction software.

It can be helpful to provide opportunities for oral rehearsal (audio recording answers before writing them down).

This learning strength can be developed through theatre sports, acting and, for some, debating. The intensity of life for some of these kids means they will seek calm and refuge in graphic novels or by creating avatars and virtual worlds in games like Minecraft.

Number smarts

Having number smarts as a learning strength is a major advantage. Developing numerical systems for organising, ordering and classifying information often suits the pattern-seeking styles of kids on the spectrums. This also increases concentration and memory as well as deepening understanding.

Obscure mathematical facts appeal to many of these kids, as does using mathematical processes to prove a theory. Some will be drawn to STEM subjects. Teaching the scientific process – research, hypothesising, experimentation and refinement of ideas or hypotheses – can also be helpful.

Try to relate numbers to physical activities: distance, speed, force or impact. Use real-world examples to help children to comprehend mathematical concepts.

Some of these neurodivergent kids may completely miss the nuance and subtlety of the symbolism in a poem but be highly skilled at interpreting symbols in advanced mathematics.

Leveraging their strengths with gizmos, tech and methods

New apps, programs and methods are powerfully re-shaping the learning experiences of neurodivergent kids. Alongside knowing their learning strengths, knowing what forms of technology can overcome a barrier to their learning or build on one of their strengths makes an amazing difference to their world. It can convert what were once insurmountable neuroproblems into neuroadvantages.

In this section I suggest gizmos that I have found helpful with neurodivergent kids. They are worth exploring.

Not every one of the gizmos mentioned will be useful or appropriate for your child, for their age range or for your budget. Please take the time to research and consider whether the gizmos are worth the time and especially the price before trying them out. I have listed these to kickstart your investigations rather than as specific recommendations for your child.

Learning
- **Articulation Station Pro.** This increases children's ability to pronounce words and sounds correctly. It was designed by speech therapists.
- **GraphoGame.** This is an academically researched learning app, game and methodology for teaching kindergarten and primary school children early literacy skills in many languages. It combines Finland's educational and special-needs expertise with evidence from cutting-edge research in neuroscience to provide one-on-one reading support.
- **Khan Academy.** This covers a range of subjects, including reading, mathematics and social-emotional learning, with the ability to pace the rate of activities to suit different learners.
- **Maths300.** This is one of the best series of maths activities that help kids create fundamental understanding of thinking in numbers. It was originally devised by our colleague Charles Lovitt. The activities range from basic understanding to sophisticated mathematical concepts.

Social
- **Social Detective.** This takes kids through a series of social scenarios and helps them decide on appropriate actions. It builds people smarts and social skills.
- **The Social Express 2.** This takes kids through a thorough social-emotional curriculum.

Calming
- **Brainwaves.** This provides the listener with 35 different programs that alter their brainwave patterns.
- **Mental Stillness.** This is a free app, well researched and effective.

Organisation and planning
- **Choiceworks.** This helps kids become more independent by helping them manage daily routines, feelings and waiting times.
- **Visual Schedule Planner.** This app helps kids on the spectrums understand and manage daily routines by creating visual schedules.

Communication

- **JASPER.** Short for Joint Attention, Symbolic Play, Engagement and Regulation, JASPER is a play-based intervention that teaches social communication skills to young children with autism. It was developed by Dr Connie Kasari at the University of California, Los Angeles.
- **More Than Words.** Developed by the Hanen Centre, this program is a parent-implemented social communication intervention for autistic children.
- **Proloquo2Go.** This enables children who are not speaking to communicate. It can be adapted for different neurodiversities.

Virtual reality (VR) and augmented reality (AR) gizmos

- **Floreo.** This is a virtual reality platform specifically designed to help neurodivergent learners develop skills.
- **Unimersiv.** This provides a variety of immersive educational experiences.

Parenting priorities for kids on the spectrums

Big impacts

- family routines made collaboratively with your child
- accepting your child and learning what they need to thrive
- attunement: adapting to the rhythm of your child's energy
- valuing their need for rest and recovery.

Quick fixes

- time in (rather than time out)
- comfort
- some direct eye contact
- playing with favourite toys.

Waste of time

- putting your child under pressure in the way other parents do (even if they find it is effective with their children)
- imposing illogical consequences
- bargaining, pleading, trying to have your child understand your perspective.

Chapter 4

Concentration and Attention Issues

The great gift of having attention issues or ADHD (attention deficit hyperactivity disorder) is a life of energy and excitement. In the long term this energy can give people an advantage in careers in business, emergency and crisis services, innovation, creative arts, sports and fitness, and skilled trades.

Life for many kids with attention issues is a bit like owning a revved-up sports car with very wayward steering and an accelerator pedal that goes from 0 to 100 in a micro-second or dawdles around all day long and seems to get nowhere.

Most of these kids have energy to burn. They rev the volume up to 11 and keep it there. They wake up early, ready to fly. Others heroically hold it together all day long and then crash into meltdowns when they get home later in the day or evening.

Some of them use almost any opportunity to ignite their excess fuel to create excitement and drama. They have differences in how they focus, delay their impulses and manage their energy levels.

Despite this, they are often mentally tired. It is a tough combination being tired and restless at the same time. The accelerator pedal is close to the floor, but it takes a lot of work to keep the steering working.

Some of these kids will have formal diagnoses of ADHD with hyperactive or impulsive actions or inattention. These are incorrectly labelled as 'deficits' or 'disorders' but are more accurately variations of the range of human experience with advantages as well as obstacles.

There are many factors that may play an important role in inattentiveness or hyperactivity, including sleep deprivation, trauma, lack of physical care or exercise, neurochemical imbalances, fear and worries about school. This is why family routines rule. There are many ways to support these kids that do not always involve medication.

The gifts of these kids include innovative thinking, the ability to think quickly, and spontaneity. In a world where many people seem weary, they stand out with bursts of excitement and energy.

Parents usually notice excessive restlessness and fidgeting or the need to move all the time between three and six years of age. For some kids, the restlessness is not behavioural but is in the mind and creates issues with hyperfocus and distractibility.

These kids are like belly buttons. Some are 'innies' and others are 'outies'. We notice the outies a lot more than the innies. That's because they are louder. Both groups have restlessness; the innies direct this inward to their own thoughts and the outies express this through their actions.

The innies

Most of the time you have no idea what is going on in the mind of innies.

When some innies try to concentrate, the level of activity in their frontal lobes decreases. Their brain turns off when it should be turning on.

In terms of learning, innies often struggle with:

- organising – they can start things but not finish them
- time management and estimation
- wandering attention
- prioritising and sequencing
- focusing and shifting attention
- sustaining effort.

These kids can be deceptive. On the surface they can appear vague and wandering, but their hyperactivity is all in their heads with thoughts scuttling along like hamsters on a treadmill.

Females with attention issues are more likely to be innies than males, but it does not always follow gender lines.

Innies are dreamy people who can appear not to listen and are more likely to obtain a diagnosis involving inattentiveness. They have short attention spans for regular events and really, really, really hate doing boring things.

The outies

Outies often receive diagnoses involving hyperactivity or impulsivity. Being an outie is like owning the sports car mentioned above but fitted with brakes that would struggle to stop a scooter.

Outies often struggle with:

- controlling their impulses
- managing when things are quiet and settled
- shame and feelings of having revealed too much about themselves.

One of the best ways to maximise well-being and resilience for both innies and outies is to help them be successful in school.

Discovering the neuroadvantages of concentration and attention issues

The brain patterns of children with attention issues commonly include variations in the functioning of:

- Dopamine levels. Almost all of these kids have low levels of dopamine, especially in the pre-frontal cortex. This is the 'get up and go' neurochemical in brains involved in rewards, motivation and executive functions.
- The basal ganglia, which regulate movements and behaviours. This can relate to starting things and stopping things.
- The ventral striatum, involved in the brain's reward system.

Another way to describe these kids is they can't stand being bored!

How parents can help

In a world where people are often casually off-hand, these kids are exuberant enthusiasts. They live their lives on the edge, but that's where the interesting things happen.

Neurodivergence tends to run in families. ADHD often runs in families. It is highly heritable, and research has identified several genetic

Neuroadvantages of kids with attention issues

Thinking and logic
- ✓ Creative
- ✓ Collect lots of ideas or facts
- ✓ List-making
- ✓ Computer games

Planning and sequencing
- ✓ Ordering
- ✓ Step-by-step planning

People smarts
- ✓ Conversation skills
- ✓ Lots of energy, get up and go
- ✓ Daring courageous friends
- ✓ Look for interesting things to do and talk about

Concentration and memory
- ✓ Passionate about areas of interest
- ✓ Hyperfocus on specific areas

Perceptual-motor skills
- ✓ Individual sports
- ✓ Martial arts
- ✓ Dance
- ✓ Drama
- ✓ Badminton
- ✓ Tennis
- ✓ Skateboarding

Language and word smarts
- ✓ Acting
- ✓ Debating
- ✓ Theatre sports
- ✓ Graphic novels

Spatial reasoning
- ✓ Artwork
- ✓ Design
- ✓ Construction
- ✓ Drawing
- ✓ Colouring in
- ✓ Trail-making

Number smarts
- ✓ Hands-on
- ✓ Estimation
- ✓ Surveying
- ✓ Mapping
- ✓ Measurement

© Andrew Fuller, *Neuroadvantage: The Strengths-based Approach to Neurodivergence* (Amba Press, 2025)

variations associated with the disorder, particularly in genes related to dopamine regulation. It can be expressed differently in boys and girls.

While neurodivergence creates advantages, it can be hard work being non-mainstream. We need to celebrate differences while also helping kids to fit in. We need to be careful to protect them from an increased risk of depression and sleep deprivation. At times their tendency to hyper-focus means they may ruminate on gloomy thoughts.

The long-term aim is not for parents to manage these kids but for them to manage themselves. While these are high-energy dynamos, they also need quiet times.

As you will see later in this chapter, several new gizmos and methods exist that help these kids to overcome challenges and to be successful.

I am yet to meet a young person with attention issues who does not have some issues with what are called 'executive functions': concentration, memory, planning, impulse control, emotional regulation and self-esteem. Part 2 of this book addresses developing these skills.

How to build your child's strengths

Highly reactive young people need more positive life events. They need teachers and parents who are the antidote to the negativity they receive.

It is highly unlikely that these kids will tell you, 'I am finding it difficult to sustain my focus and concentration in class.' Instead, they will most likely declare, 'School is boring!'

Living with these kids is challenging. Some don't settle and they don't sleep for long. For some, the completion of an hour of homework takes four hours with screaming. They live in messy rooms, write work projects in erratic handwriting and have chaotic life schedules. Parenting them is like trying to hold on to a wriggling salmon.

Eventually we want children with attention issues to develop the self-awareness to increase their ability to concentrate and increase outputs.

Some of the things some of the children I have worked with have found helpful include:

- lamps that give the 'right' amount of lighting for them
- headphones to minimise noise and distractions
- fidget toys
- a movable chair

- a step under the desk to raise their feet
- a standing desk
- notepads and pens
- water
- sticky notes
- a timer.

Step 1: Find their learning strengths

Learning strengths can help to direct children's efforts towards their areas of strength. Complete the analysis of learning strengths at www.mylearningstrengths.com and use the free letter to create a conversation about building on the identified strengths. Discuss these with your child's teacher(s). A full report is also available outlining strategies, strengths and possible future career areas.

Step 2: Build on their learning strengths

We create success for our children when we start from what is strong.

Use your child's top two learning strengths and combine this knowledge with the information below to start building their neuroadvantage.

To be distracted is to be attracted (usually by something other than what other people think the kid should be focusing on) – knowing what draws their attention helps.

Spatial reasoning

While the innies might be completing an artwork, design project or jigsaw puzzle, outies might be constructing something in the back yard or designing an awesome skatepark.

Thinking in pictures is often a learning strength, as these kids often think more powerfully in images than in long strands of words. Using visuals rather than words, drawing, colouring, trail-making, and joining the dots are some ways they can settle. Creating schedules with different colours for different activities can be helpful.

Increasing this learning strength will also promote their ability to 'read' other people.

Perceptual-motor skills

These kids often prefer doing things rather than sitting back and reflecting on things. This can make school a total boredom-fest for some. Their high-octane energy levels mean they are usually keen on physical activities and sports. Long-term, they have all the get-up-and-go, vitality and persistence to be successful.

Individual sports will suit some of them more than team sports, where higher levels of people smarts and verbal negotiation are required.

Innies might be more drawn to mastering a dance routine or a skateboard manoeuvre, while outies might be more inclined to be assembling a drum kit.

Dance, table tennis, badminton, martial arts movements, rapid tai chi, finger-movement games and standing or walking will usually help these kids to focus or settle.

Computer games such as Minecraft, Pokémon GO, Wii Zumba Fitness, Dance Dance Revolution and Fitness Boxing may also be helpful.

Some will seek out sensations if they feel distressed, others will avoid closeness and react powerfully if someone invades their personal space, and others will use physical means to distract themselves.

Concentration and memory

While we often think of these kids as having wandering attention, some can have laser-like focus on things that really engross them. Sadly, this doesn't just apply to positive thoughts. Some of them can dwell and brood for far too long on negative thoughts.

Exercise, if you can get them to do it, will help some. Some of them get into table tennis or rock climbing or roller blading. Just make sure you don't call it exercise or sport.

Others will benefit from reminders on devices to keep track of time and to remind them to shift to different activities or tasks. They need consistency but also need stimulation to pay attention. The aim is a state of relaxed, alert stimulation.

Their heightened stress hormones decrease immunity, and activity in their hippocampus can result in patchy memory.

Binaural beats, puzzles, memory quizzes, doodling, knitting and fidget spinners are some ways of helping these kids focus and learn. Use timers and create short-burst tasks so that completion of activities becomes a game.

We often think about mindfulness as a process of slowing and calming. For some of these kids, the more quickly experiences happen, the more able they are to focus and be engaged. Many of them relax through speed rather than stillness.

Planning and sequencing

Even with strengths in this area, these kids often take a crisis-management approach to life. They seek out adrenaline. The moment is what matters to them.

Some of them are *just-in-time managers* who complete tasks at the last possible micro-second before something is due. Others are *masters of minimalism* who, if asked by a teacher to write 50 words on a topic, feel they have seriously overdone it if they have written 51 words.

Organisational skills are often a bit chaotic, and they struggle to follow through. While they are at school, it can be best for parents to strongly take the lead on the business side of getting things done all the way through to school completion.

It can be better to have several tasks or activities on the go at the same time to increase variety (and stimulation).

As mentioned earlier, take a load off these kids' minds by giving choices: 'Would you like to do … first or … first?' If they refuse those, add another option and repeat: 'So would you like to do … (new option) or … or … first?' Outline the options and let them make decisions.

Help them get in the practice of making to-do lists and making notes.

Creating project planners that outline each step towards an outcome and prioritising the steps helps them to use this learning strength to actively create success.

Most of these kids underachieve at school because of variable concentration. However, they are able to develop vice-like focus on things that fascinate them.

While these kids can be quite physical, they can also be quite accident-prone. Developing this learning strength through sport, rock wall climbing, martial arts or high-intensity training benefits their learning. (You may want to read and consider the section on 'Primitive reflexes' in Chapter 7.)

Have them keep a folder with a separate section for each subject and make sure everything that goes into the notebook is put in the correct section. Keep subjects colour-coded.

Lego blocks, chess, backgammon, badminton, table tennis, SimCity, Minecraft and Monument Valley will help these kids to learn.

Thinking and logic

Developing this learning strength is a great advantage for both innies and outies. They are able to think clearly and logically, but almost invariably they act before they think, which leads to problems in learning and in life.

We need to have strategies for helping them have their actions align with their intellect. As outies are often dramatic and conflict-seeking, some will love the 'cut and thrust' of debates and philosophical disputes. Innies may prefer discussions about ethical approaches to social issues.

Forensic sciences may interest some; logic puzzles and ethical dilemmas can also help develop these learning strengths. Chess is the best game for the improvement of strategic and logical thinking. Code Hero, Portal and Portal 2, Uno, checkers, dominoes and 20 Questions are also great strategy and thinking-type games.

Some kids who are distractible and prone to daydreaming are incredibly creative and innovative and can find links between ideas that do not occur to many people. These are the sorts of skills found in writers, film producers and scriptwriters.

Help them work out the most important thing to attend to. The world is overwhelming if you try to pay attention to everything. They need to learn to prioritise, to pick out the main idea.

People smarts

A common misunderstanding is that neurodivergent kids always have poor interpersonal skills. This is not true. Some are highly tuned into others, pick up on the feelings of others accurately, are deeply sensitive and are great friends.

Some can become incredibly sensitive to fears of being rejected by friends (sometimes called 'rejection sensitivity') and become anxious and lose confidence in their own judgment in social settings. Others may be more likely to express this by becoming oppositional. For these kids, moods and negativity are highly contagious. Be the positive antidote.

An accepting peer group is essential for these kids to develop people smarts.

Cynicism and sarcasm are destructive forces in these kids' lives. Never use them.

Developing some skills in this area pays off. Kids can be extremely competent in other areas, but if they lack the basic skills to work in with others, success can elude them. It can be difficult to make and keep friends without an inner 'brake' that helps them to think, 'Maybe that is not the best thing to say right now.'

Some of these kids have interpersonal problems because it is generally not helpful to say to other people everything you think. Their energy and impulsivity can be seen by others as rudeness and thoughtlessness.

Learning 'people reading' and conversational skills is a major long-term advantage.

Language and word smarts

This learning strength can be developed through theatre sports, acting and debating. The intensity of life for some of these kids means they seek calm and refuge in comics, cartoons and graphic novels. Innies may become great lovers of books and movies. Others write and illustrate diaries and notes. Many great poets and quite a few songwriters are neurodivergent.

Word games, crossword puzzles, find-the-word games, graphic novels and Wordle are just some of the activities that develop this further.

Some neurodivergent kids become avid readers, as it helps them to understand mysteries in their personal world.

Number smarts

Relate numbers to activities: distance, speed, force, impact. You will often get further in this area by assisting the outies or active kids to develop trails, jumps and skate ramps than by talking about numbers abstractly. Try to include a physical option outdoors wherever you can.

Estimation games, measurement activities, surveying, mapping and Sudoku will all help these kids to focus.

Games such as Slenderman, Flappy Bird, Tap the Frog and Ant Smasher will help these kids to recognise their emotional reactions to different experiences and develop awareness of the physiological component of emotions.

The computer game Farming Simulator is good for stretching number smarts. It allows players to work as farmers who raise livestock and grow and sell crops to earn money. Players can control farm machinery and breed animals in the game.

Leveraging their strengths with gizmos, tech and methods

Please remember that I am not trying to provide a complete list but am just pointing you to a few things I have found helpful for kids with attention issues.

Learning

Create a quiet learning or study space with minimal distractions. As these kids hate monotony, break tasks down into brief parts and challenge them to get as much done as possible by a set time. Use a stopwatch or sand clock, increasing the amount of time to focus on an activity. Wobble chairs, standing desks and movement help with hyperactivity. Movement supports concentration.

Computers and artificial intelligence can play a wonderful role in the lives of these kids. Being able to store information on a hard disk can help kids who would otherwise present as vague and distracted. For this reason, parents can help them to organise information on their laptops by creating specific files for major areas such as each school subject.

- **Alarmy.** This is an alarm clock app with various challenges that force the user to wake up and start their day. It's useful for students who struggle with getting up in the morning or transitioning between tasks.
- **Dragon NaturallySpeaking.** This is speech-to-text software that allows kids to dictate their notes, assignments or emails. It's particularly helpful for kids who find typing or writing challenging.
- **Evernote.** This is a versatile note-taking app that allows students to organise notes, to-do lists and ideas. It also includes features for scanning documents, saving web pages, and organising information by tags and notebooks.

- **Focus Booster.** This is an app based on the Pomodoro Technique, which involves working for a set period (typically 25 minutes) followed by a short break.
- **Notion.** A powerful all-in-one workspace, this combines note-taking, task management and collaboration features. It's highly customisable and can be used for organising study notes, to-do lists and project plans.
- **OneNote.** Microsoft's note-taking app, this integrates with other Microsoft Office tools. It allows students to create and organise notes, draw or type, and sync across devices.

Calming

The calming gizmos that work are often more active than the mental stillness, guided-relaxation types of applications:

- Ant Smasher
- bubble-popping games
- popping bubble wrap
- Zones of Regulation
- GoNoodle for movement breaks.

Organisation and planning

Use picture planners, whiteboards and noticeboards at home.

Simplify: have fewer folders, less paper, less clothing, less stuff. Minimalism helps these kids.

- **Goblin Tools.** This is a collection of small, simple, single-task tools, mostly designed to help neurodivergent people with tasks they find overwhelming or difficult. For kids who become anxious and don't know where to begin, it will put the steps into a spinning wheel and then suggest a starting point. Invaluable.
- **Google Calendar.** This is a calendar app that allows kids to schedule tasks, set reminders and share their calendar with others. It helps to keep track of daily schedules and upcoming deadlines.
- **Habitica.** A habit-building and productivity app that gamifies daily tasks, this is designed to help students build good habits and track progress by turning tasks into a role-playing game.

- **Magic ToDo.** This is a Goblin Tool that breaks things down so you don't.
- **Remember the Milk.** This creates a to-do list on your phone.
- **Todoist.** A task-management app that helps kids organise tasks and assignments, this allows users to set due dates, prioritise tasks, and break down large projects into smaller steps.
- **Trello.** A visual project management tool, this uses boards, lists and cards to organise tasks. It's useful for students who benefit from seeing their tasks laid out visually.

Chunk it up and break it down

Use clear, short verbal instructions made one at a time. Where possible back these up with a visual.

Parenting priorities for kids with attention issues

Big impacts

- try to make things fast (but not furious)
- have structured and predictable routines
- break tasks into smaller steps
- base learning on interest and strength areas
- develop a 'what to do if I'm feeling bored' strategy that doesn't involve disrupting someone else
- try concentration training
- get enough sleep
- build a culture of co-operation in your family.

Quick fixes

- focus on their area of interest or learning strength
- encourage movement and physical activity.

Waste of time

- following well-meaning but often misguided advice that results in you feeling under pressure to parent in the way other parents do
- bribery
- arguing over issues that don't really matter

- having too many rules
- demanding respect.

If it's not one thing, it could also be another

There are some groupings of neurodiversity that can overlap in some kids. They can be on the spectrums and also have attention issues. This is quite a common overlap. When these two challenges overlap, parents need to plan carefully.

- Think about when, where and how your child communicates best.
- Help them to express their needs as clearly as possible.
- Identify triggers for upsets. Look for patterns.
- Try to develop a calm-down routine. This can become quicker over time, but don't rush it.

Similarities between attention issues and the spectrums	
Strengths	- Individual approaches to problem-solving - Passionate interests - Detailed thinking - Resilience
Challenges	- Managing frustrations - Don't react to sudden changes well - Making and keep friends - Usually have areas of executive functions that need to be developed (see Part 2 of this book) - Can find it difficult to calm themselves down - Rigid 'Velcro' ideas - Difficulty with abstract concepts

Chapter 5

Sensitivities and Sensory Processing Issues

It is not always easy to be sensitive and highly attuned. The gifts of this condition include an amplified awareness, a connection to the environment, enhanced perception, deep presence and unique creative and emotional insights.

In the long term, these gifts are often highly desired in careers in the intersection between technology and the arts, film-making, communication, animal care, culinary arts and landscape design.

If you have ever had an itch you couldn't quite reach to scratch, you'll know how preoccupying it can be. Now imagine all of your nerve endings on full alert and you may be able to comprehend a little of the intensity of sensation these kids experience.

Their heightened sensitivity can relate to the brightness of light, volume of sound, touch, smell or tastes. Sensitivity can also relate to their own bodies. When kids are overwhelmed by their senses, they can be less tuned in to their movements and can appear clumsy or to have poor balance. Chapter 7 discusses movement issues. Some of these kids may be diagnosed with sensory processing disorder.

Others can be under-responsive to sensory information and may not react as most people would to pain, discomfort or danger. Some of these kids engage in rocking or spinning to create more intense sensory experiences that help them feel more relaxed and grounded.

Some are *sensory seeking* and like specific textures, shapes or aromas. Often their learning is enhanced when they can move around, have crunchy snacks, use fidget spinners, chew on drink bottles, or wear textural clothing. It might be helpful for such kids to learn to spell by writing in chalk on paths outdoors.

Others are *sensory avoiders* who become overwhelmed when they perceive the world too vividly or intensely and need time out with minimal stimulation. Some will try to reduce the impact of their senses by wearing hats and sunglasses indoors, preferring places with low lighting, using earbuds, and only eating foods they know they like. Others will need soft-fabric clothing with labels cut off.

Others are *sensory distractors* who act in interesting ways to divert their sensory overload.

Knowing the sensory patterns of these kids helps them to maintain an appropriate level of arousal so they can learn.

Clothing and discomfort are big issues for some of these kids. Some fabrics, clothing tags, washing detergents or materials irritate and overwhelm them. Schools with rigid policies around uniforms are a nightmare. Helping them to get dressed can be like engaging in tag-team wrestling.

While we mostly see sensitivity to external objects – textures, aromas, clothing – it can also be emotional. Many of these kids also experience 'rejection sensitivity', which is a heightened response to perceived or real rejection. This is something we see in kids on the spectrums, with attention issues, anxiety and lowered moods.

The gifts of sensory sensitivities set these kids up to get the highs as well as the lows of life.

Discovering the neuroadvantages of sensory processing issues

We all have to filter out sensory feelings that aren't related to what we are currently doing. For example, for much of the day we are unaware of the feeling of shoes on our feet.

The brain patterns of children with sensory processing issues commonly include variations in the functioning of:

- the sensory filters, which work differently in these kids, which can cause sensory overload or distraction

- the somatosensory cortex, which processes touch and body awareness
- the thalamus, a brain region that acts as a relay station for sensory information
- white matter tracts, which consist of nerve fibres that connect different parts of the brain and facilitate communication between them.

How parents can help

These kids often have challenges in areas related to sensory perception, integration and regulation. Trying to function while being overwhelmed by sensory experiences can be exhausting, especially if they are stressed.

- **Sensitivity to sounds.** Generally these kids are easily distracted because almost every irrelevant sound is amplified. One condition called hyperacusis involves extreme sensitivity to sounds. As one kid explained, 'It's like I can hear ants breathe.'
- **Sensitivity to foods.** Most kids I have seen have strong aversions to particular foods and food textures. The foods some of them can 'stomach' are so limited that without vitamin supplementation they would have extreme nutritional deficiencies.
- **Sensitivity to clothing.** Labels, textures and fabrics, as well as specific laundry detergents that would leave most of unbothered, are intolerable to these kids.
- **Vomiting.** For some kids, the queasy feeling in their tummies becomes an overwhelming fear of vomiting. This often leads to them avoiding some situations or experiencing extreme panic when they have feelings of nausea.

Parents need to be like detectives working out which stimuli distress their child and which comfort them. Eventually this will enable the child to advocate for themselves and to ensure the environment they work or live in is suitable for them.

As you will see later in this chapter, several new gizmos and methods exist that help these kids to overcome challenges and to be successful.

Neuroadvantages of kids with sensory processing issues

Planning and sequencing
- ✓ Pair steps in a sequence with pleasant sensations
- ✓ Intensity of feelings can make the most intense issues the most pressing

Thinking and logic
- ✓ Creative
- ✓ Adaptable
- ✓ Flexible

Concentration and memory
- ✓ Engrossed in areas of interest
- ✓ Strong memory
- ✓ Need comfort to focus

People smarts
- ✓ Kind and caring
- ✓ Good friendship skills

Perceptual-motor skills
- ✓ Sensitive awareness of environment

Language and word smarts
- ✓ Able to write and communicate in vivid, imagery-rich language

Spatial reasoning
- ✓ Spatial awareness
- ✓ Visual reasoning
- ✓ Aesthetics
- ✓ Visual design

Number smarts
- ✓ Clarity of numbers appeals

© Andrew Fuller, *Neuroadvantage: The Strengths-based Approach to Neurodivergence* (Amba Press, 2025)

Step 1: Find their learning strengths

As described earlier, go to www.mylearningstrengths.com and complete the analysis, either with them or on their behalf.

Step 2: Build on their learning strengths

We create success for our children when we start from what is strong. Use your child's top two learning strengths and combine this knowledge with the information.

Spatial reasoning

The sensitivity of these kids can be dreadfully preoccupying but can also have an upside: awareness. Often, their ability to think in pictures allows them to excel in tasks that involve visual reasoning, design and spatial awareness. Some will be able to convert their unique sensory experiences into inspiration for artistic and innovative work.

These kids often have an enhanced appreciation for aesthetics, particularly in environments that cater to their sensory preferences, such as nature, art or music.

Perceptual-motor skills

These kids' heightened sensory awareness allows them to notice subtle details in their environment that others might overlook.

It is necessary to cater for the exquisitely tuned sense these kids have. It is a bit like Goldilocks: not too hot, not too cold, not too bright, not too dim.

Stability balls and wobble chairs can be useful at school. One way to help with sensory overload is overloading the senses. While lowering the amount of stimulation a kid gets makes intuitive sense, sometimes the reverse is true. This is usually a one-off attempt that will either work well or not work out at once. One try, and you will know. For example, people with pronounced gag reflexes often cope better during dental procedures when salt is placed on the back of their tongues. For this reason, finding stress balls, specific fabrics and fidget toys can help kids to self-regulate in different environments.

Concentration and memory

When not overwhelmed by sensory distractions, these kids focus well. They almost always have exceptional memories, particularly for sensory details, and exhibit a high level of attention to detail in tasks that align with their sensory preferences.

They can become deeply engrossed in tasks or activities that they find stimulating.

Planning and sequencing

Use sensory materials that they like to represent the steps in a plan and lay them out in order. These can be colours, fabrics, textures or sounds.

Thinking and logic

Often these kids feel first then use logic. They are often intuitive. Their sensitivity gives them access to novel ideas and artistic expression. This creativity can be particularly evident in fields such as music, visual arts and writing. They have strong problem-solving skills and adaptability.

The intensity of their sensory world can play havoc with clear thinking. Take time to consider the ideal learning and thinking environment for your child.

People smarts

Sensitivity doesn't just apply to foods, fabrics and sound; these kids are highly attuned to their own feelings as well as the feelings of others. Generally, they have high levels of emotional intelligence. Many show strong empathy and emotional sensitivity, allowing them to connect deeply with others and understand their feelings.

Some of these kids are so sensory-seeking that they not only like people, they want to touch them. Helping them learn social boundaries and personal distance is important in developing social skills.

Language and word smarts

These kids' awareness of the sensory world can enable them to express themselves in rich and vivid language.

Number smarts

The non-sensory world of numbers can almost seem like a refuge for some of these kids.

Leveraging their strengths with gizmos, tech and methods

Learning

Sensory play is a vital feature of helping these kids to learn without distraction. What might appear as distracted fiddling by other kids is actually calming and focusing for these kids.

Noise-cancelling headphones or earbuds are often helpful.

- **Dexteria.** This is an app that provides therapeutic hand exercises to improve fine motor skills and sensory processing. Activities designed to enhance hand strength, dexterity and coordination are useful for students with sensory processing issues who have motor skill challenges.
- **Kurzweil 3000.** An assistive technology tool that provides reading, writing and study support for students with learning differences, this includes text-to-speech, word prediction, and study aids that help with reading comprehension, note-taking and writing.
- **OT Play.** This is a collection of activities designed by occupational therapists to improve sensory processing and motor skills in children. It includes guided activities that focus on sensory integration, fine motor skills and coordination.
- **Sensory App House.** This is a collection of apps designed to provide sensory input and stimulation through visual and auditory experiences. These apps focus on different sensory experiences, such as lights, sounds and interactive visualisations.
- **SoundAMP.** This app enhances sound for users who are either under-responsive to auditory input or need specific sounds amplified while background noise is filtered out. It provides real-time sound amplification with the ability to adjust the frequency and volume of different sounds.
- **White Noise.** This app provides background sounds to mask environmental noises that might be distracting or overwhelming for

students with sensory processing issues. It includes a wide range of soundscapes, from white noise to nature sounds, that can help create a calming auditory environment.

Calming

Swimming, yoga, martial arts, gymnastics and GymbaROO can be wonderful ways of calming kids.

Lowered lighting and weighted blankets also help.

Therapeutic compression clothing (for example, Squease or SmartKnitKIDS) provides calming deep-pressure input, which can help students with sensory processing issues feel more grounded and focused. It is discreet, wearable clothing that delivers consistent, gentle compression.

Patricia Wilbarger has developed a series of activities designed to meet sensory needs. This includes jumping on a mini-trampoline, using fidget toys, placing pool noodles at their feet, pushing heavy objects and using large muscle groups. A helpful outline can be found at www.x-fragile.be/wp-content/uploads/XF-Miami-095.pdf.

The Wilbarger brushing protocol is a sensory technique to reduce hypersensitivity to touch.

A sensory space is a controlled environment that provides sensory experiences to help people regulate their emotions and behaviours. Activities like climbing, squeezing putty, spinning or rocking help with balance and coordination.

There are companies that design sensory-friendly clothing with soft fabrics, seamless designs and no tags. Sensory toothbrushes are also available for kids with dental sensitivities.

- **Calm Counter.** This is a visual and audio tool for helping children manage anger and frustration. It uses a simple 'I need a break' timer, which can be helpful for students who need to step away from overwhelming situations. A calming sequence with visual and auditory cues helps children de-escalate their emotions.
- **Headspace for Kids.** This mindfulness app offers guided meditation and relaxation exercises tailored for children, helping them manage stress and sensory overload. The meditation sessions are specifically designed for focus, relaxation and sleep.

Organisation and planning
- **Choiceworks.** This visual schedule app helps students with sensory sensitivities to understand and manage daily routines and make transitions between activities.
- **Visual Timer.** A visual countdown timer, this helps kids to manage time and understand how much time is left for an activity. A large, visual countdown display shows the passage of time in a clear, easily understandable way.

Virtual reality (VR) and augmented reality (AR)
First Then Visual Schedule. This is a visual schedule app designed to help students understand sequences of activities, which is particularly beneficial for those who struggle with transitions or need structure. It offers customisable visual schedules with the ability to add images, videos and voice recordings.

Parenting priorities for kids with sensory processing sensitivities
Big impacts
- structured routines
- working out the right environment for your child
- sensory spaces and the right sensory 'diet' for your child
- social skills training.

Quick fixes
- using large muscle groups
- pressure
- fabrics, textures and feelings associated with comfort.

Waste of time
- talking these kids out of their sensitivities
- dismissing the validity of their feelings
- forcing them to tolerate sensations that distress them.

If it's not one thing, it could also be another

Similarities between sensory processing issues and the spectrums	
Strengths	- Thinking involving patterns and systems - Creative thinking - Attention to detail - Logical problem-solving
Challenges	- Sensory overload - Difficulty making and keeping friends - Executive functions - Calming emotions - Ability to think about abstract ideas and concepts
Similarities between sensory processing and attention issues	
Strengths	- High energy and enthusiasm - Passionate enthusiasm for specific areas of interest - Innovative and creative problem-solving
Challenges	- Distractibility - Can become overwhelmed by environmental conditions: temperature, lighting, sound - Impulse control

Chapter 6
Arguments and Defiance

The gifts of defiance are resolute individualism and tenacious determination. In the long term these gifts provide people with a leverage in careers in the law and justice, business, lobbying, politics, defence forces and sports.

If you ever have to go into battle, you will want one of these kids on your side. If you have a group of these kids on your team, your chances of winning are overwhelmingly good. They know what is right, what is fair and exactly how to stand up and argue for it.

If you really insist on arguing with them (not recommended), these neurodivergent kids can be 'tricky'. They can dispute, defy and dismiss even seemingly minor requests. Up to 16 per cent of children and teens meet the diagnostic criteria for oppositional defiant disorder (ODD). Labelling this as a 'disorder' is incorrect, because when they are supported well by parents and teachers, these kids can make constructive improvements to injustices in the world.

These gifts set these kids up to take on and change the world.

Discovering the neuroadvantages of defiance

The brain patterns of children with defiance commonly include variations in the functioning of:

- the amygdala, which is overactive, increasing the intensity and reactivity of fear and anger and frustrations
- the anterior cingulate gyrus, which is also overactive, which can cause children to repeat the same behaviours in the same way over

and over again (The anterior cingulate gyrus helps us to modify our behaviours in different contexts, something some kids with defiance find challenging. This means that transition points in homes – getting to bed on time, getting ready for school etc. – can be flare-up points. This can also interfere with understanding consequences.)
- the temporal lobes (above our ears), which help us to interpret the intentions of other people accurately (Kids with defiance can perceive hostility when none is present.)
- the frontal lobes, which are involved in controlling our initial impulses and making good decisions.

These kids have formidable strengths. They are strong-willed, determined young people with a powerful sense of purpose and conviction.

Their neurodivergence is often expressed as an 'all or nothing' mindset. They can be determined in their thinking, patchy in persistence and explosive when things don't work out. No learning occurs for them if the relationships they have with teachers and parents are not supportive.

While these kids are often bright, their academic results do not always reflect this. Success at school can be challenging because schools like to implement consequences for behavioural indiscretions. If one of these kids doesn't agree that a rule is just or fair, they will argue tooth and nail. As a result, some of these kids spend an inordinate amount of their time at school in time-out rooms, on detention or outside the office.

They often say, 'You can't make me', and the truth is, they are right.

These reactions alone create enough obstacles to learning, but an avoidant fear of failure is also common among these kids.

How parents can help

Parents cringe when receiving calls from the school. They also receive disapproving glances and misguided advice from relatives and other parents. The gist of those messages is 'Toughen up and make your child comply'. *This is not only wrong – it is damaging.*

In my book *Tricky Kids* I described these kids as having the 'Winston Churchill syndrome' – defiant, strong and resolute. Generally, kids don't tell lies; they make up stories to protect themselves.

Parents can't battle their way towards behavioural compliance with these kids. Creating a version of World War 3 in your family home is *not* the solution.

To expand on a point made in Chapter 1, our brains have two main feeling pathways:

The first of these is activated by the amygdala and usually leads to feelings of stress, fear and pain. The stress hormones of cortisol and adrenaline are elevated.

Some common parenting statements that activate this feeling pathway are:

- If you don't stop that … (insert threat or consequence)
- Why are you doing that?
- Why haven't you … (finished your homework/walked the dog/put out the rubbish)?
- Just you wait till your father gets home!

I'm sure you can recall a few lines from your own childhood.

The second feeling pathway is activated by the hypothalamus and the pituitary gland, which are releasing oxytocin and vasopressin. These are the hormones of trust, connection and belonging.

Some common parenting statements that activate this pathway are:

- Are you ok?
- What's going on for you? You are not usually like this.
- What is the matter? What has happened?

While many people think that the amygdala pathway is needed for parents to contain behaviour, with many kids and especially with oppositional kids the second pathway is much more powerful in changing behaviour and ensuring long-term life success.

Dealing with setbacks

These kids do not deal well with the frustration of things not working out the way they hoped. Helping them learn to deal with setbacks is an essential lesson. Sadly, chucking a wobbly and demanding that you get your own way is rarely well received in the adult world of work.

The best way to deal with a setback is to step forward. When a setback inevitably occurs, start by acknowledging their feelings: 'It's really frustrating when things don't go the way we hope.'

If they are open to it, provide comfort and reassurance. Hugs and touch are great for some kids, but you will be the best judge of whether your child responds well to this.

Some kids need time to brood before they are ready to talk. Ask: 'Would you like to talk about it now or later?'

It is often better to separate the reaction to the setback from the planning. When we are frustrated or disappointed, we are rarely at our most creative or thinking flexibly.

When they are ready, you can have a conversation using some of the following questions or statements:

- It's really disappointing when things don't work out. How did you feel?
- Just because it didn't work out this time doesn't mean we can't make it work out.
- What do you think we could try differently next time? Let's think about all of the different ways we could try to make this happen.
- What else could we try? (You could write ideas on a piece of paper or a small whiteboard.)
- Would you mind if I suggested an idea?
- Is there anything we can learn from this setback?

The automatic 'no'

One of the common features of kids who like to argue is that they are 'stuck'. 'Stuckness' is a characteristic of people with obsessions, ruminative worries, gambling problems, addictions and long-standing grudges and feuds. Where you will most often see this in before- and after-school care is when these kids become incredibly oppositional. They want to argue.

They are often legendary kids. Their first word is 'No'. Their first phrase is 'I don't have to' and their first full sentence is 'You can't make me – you are not the boss of me!'

Often they will argue about the same things over and over again. They can get so focused on an issue or incident that they can't get beyond it. If you ever say to them something like, 'It seems to me that you argue with everything I say', they will hotly reply, 'No I don't!'

How arguments can be a good thing

Healthy families can have arguments. Often conflict highlights the need for change and growth. It is the way families argue rather than the arguing itself that makes the difference.

One of the ways of thinking about a family is that it is a bit like a debating competition. One team want things to change; the other team want things to stay the same.

The change team (usually the kids) say things like	The stay the same team (usually the parents) say things like
I want to go out more	It's a school night
I need more pocket money	You know what your allowance is
I want to leave school	You need to finish your schooling
I'm going to a party	We need to call their parents
My girlfriend or boyfriend is staying over	You're not old enough
Everybody else is allowed to	Everyone else is not my responsibility
All the other parents let their kids …	I don't care what other parents do

It is through debating these sorts of issues that families grow up and develop. While differences of opinion and disputes can be useful, they can also leave you gasping and exhausted if you are not careful.

In the middle of our brains is a part called the 'anterior cingulate gyrus', and when this becomes overactivated people do the same things over and over again.

If you say to them	They are likely to reply with
Do you like arguing?	No.
Do you like people being upset with you?	No.
Do you like it when people threaten consequences?	No.
So then why do you do it?	I don't know.

They are being honest with us. They really don't know.

It is easy to misinterpret these kids' behaviours (wrongly) as lazy, rude, disrespectful.

Let's now return to their learning strengths.

The daunting task of engaging these kids in learning can cause parents and teachers to lower their expectations of them. This is a mistake. These kids are often very clever and can be highly successful. One of the most powerful ways to increase the well-being and resilience of these kids is to keep engaging them in learning and school. Connection beats coercion hands down.

These kids find focus, calm and success in high-adrenaline, high-challenge environments that interest them. If you are wanting to take these kids on holidays, do not take them to an isolated desert island with nothing to do, as they will drive you crazy.

Several new gizmos and methods exist that help these kids to overcome challenges and to be successful.

Step 1: Find their learning strengths

A way to help them is, when they are calm, to invite them to complete the analysis of their learning strengths at www.mylearningstrengths.com.

If you can't persuade them to do it, you (their parent) should complete the analysis on their behalf. The result will help guide your efforts either way.

The free letter will be helpful, but with these kids consider purchasing the full Personalised Learning Success Plan. Start with what is strong and then see if you can help them to transfer those abilities into other areas.

Step 2: Build on their learning strengths

We create success for our children when we start from what is strong.

Use your child's top two learning strengths and combine this knowledge with the information below to start building their neuroadvantage.

Spatial reasoning

Artistic skills are quite common with these kids. They often like to draw. Some will also be attracted to action figures, Minecraft and manga. Computer games give them dopamine hits, a sense of control and a place to express strong emotions. Again, we have to keep in mind the risk of

Neuroadvantages of kids with defiance

Planning and sequencing
✓ Imagine forwards, plan backwards

Thinking and logic
✓ Methodical thinking

People smarts
✓ Doing activities with people
✓ Sports
✓ Gymnastics
✓ Skateboarding

Concentration and memory
✓ Verbal concentration

Defiance

Language and word smarts
✓ Action stories
✓ Create your own adventures

Perceptual-motor skills
✓ Walking
✓ Fishing
✓ Table tennis
✓ Martial arts
✓ Badminton

Spatial reasoning
✓ Drawing
✓ Manga
✓ Ballistics
✓ Trajectories

Number smarts
✓ Probability thinking

© Andrew Fuller, *Neuroadvantage: The Strengths-based Approach to Neurodivergence* (Amba Press, 2025)

computer games becoming overly relied upon. Their use should always be part of a balanced life.

Building from this into spatial reasoning might require investigating ballistics, trajectories of projectiles, or movement of figures across terrain.

Perceptual-motor skills

Kids with learning strengths in perceptual-motor skills are often drawn towards action and doing things rather than thinking them over too deeply. Pairing ideas with movements, talking to them while walking beside them, asking them to point to main ideas or sometimes to act out a concept can be helpful.

Musical training often benefits these kids (especially drumming), as does team sports. Fishing, golf, badminton and martial arts can also be successful.

Concentration and memory

While these kids might display the detailed memory of a constitutional lawyer in the midst of a dispute, concentration is not often their main learning strength. Two issues are often present:

1. a tendency to over-focus on an aspect of something, and
2. being easily distracted.

Prompting them, gently, to determine what is the most important issue or task and then focus on it helps. It is also useful to help them to learn to shift their concentration from focused and narrow to broader and panoramic where they can consider a wider range of perspectives.

Planning and sequencing

Oppositional kids tend to be more reactive than proactive. For this reason, planning can be an undiscovered learning strength. Parents should aim to develop their child's intentions, not just their ability to argue. Setting plans and schedules to achieve outcomes they deem to be worthwhile is a great opportunity to develop in this area.

Help them to learn to 'imagine forwards and plan backwards'. This involves defining a goal or outcome they want and then specifying the steps needed to create that result.

You may find that they plan more easily by using Post-it notes for each of the steps.

Thinking and logic

Applying their logic in the heat of a dispute is often second nature to these kids. Applying thinking and logic in a cool-headed, methodical way is sometimes less developed.

Oppositional kids can develop learning strengths in thinking and logic by using thinking routines. These help them to tune in to their own self-talk and develop the skills of self-questioning.

These are set questions that help them to analyse situations and their thoughts:

- What is the most important thing?
- What am I telling myself about this?
- What am I feeling about it?
- Should I believe that my feeling is right?
- What am I sure about? What am I less certain of?
- Are there any other points of view I could consider?
- What is the outcome I would like?
- What are some ways that could happen?
- What is the best way?

People smarts

This is usually an area of major challenge for these kids, but their future success requires developing some people smarts.

One of the most important people smarts to develop is curiosity. Considering that other people may see things differently, think in alternative ways, and even feel differently, is a vital life skill.

Kids with tricky behaviours are often exceptionally loyal to the people they trust.

Unfortunately, they are more likely to interpret people they don't know or trust as hostile.

Helping them to work out who to trust and discussing with them how to determine trustworthiness is important to the development of people smarts. The best way to learn to trust is by being with people who are trustworthy – people who are reliable, do what they say they are going to do, show up for them, start each day afresh and forgive yesterday's issues, and build connections through interests and learning strengths.

These kids possess the people smarts that give them the capacity to be constructive leaders. Empower them and give them important roles at school and at home.

Developing the art of calming down is essential. The world is not always a fair and just place, and losing your cool over every injustice is not effective.

Language and word smarts

These kids can be extremely articulate when angry but monosyllabic when morose or sullen. As such, their strengths in language and word smarts vary.

The passive nature of reading will be intolerable to some of these kids, who may prefer films, YouTube clips and game-based ways of learning.

This, however, is not true of all kids with defiance. Some find the safety of an imaginary world in a book to be comforting and calming. Utilise the wonderful skills of librarians to find the right book, film or game.

Number smarts

It is essential for these kids to learn about probability. Learning to weigh up options and consider the probability of different outcomes sets them up for success.

For example:

If I yell out at my teacher, what is the probability that I will get what I want? Not sure. 50/50

In the short term? Maybe. 70/30

In the long term? No. 0/100

Probability thinking links to percentages of chances, and developing this skill applies number smarts to being able to control your impulses.

Most of us have access to probability charts every day in the form of weather forecasts. What is the likelihood or probability of rain today?

Kids with defiance will not be perfect in applying probability thinking (very few of us are). Nevertheless, helping them to go through a process of considering probabilities for the big decisions in their life will make a major difference.

In summary, because these kids present challenges doesn't mean they can't succeed at school. By learning to build on what they are already good at, they can be helped to grow in other areas, and their experience of success will develop their confidence and self-esteem.

Leveraging their strengths with gizmos, tech and methods

Learning
- **Khan Academy.** This provides a self-paced, personalised learning platform that students can navigate independently, which may appeal to those who resist traditional instruction.
- **Quizlet.** This tool allows students to create or access flashcards and study sets in a fun and interactive way, enabling them to take more ownership of their learning.

Calming
- **Breathe, Think, Do with Sesame.** An app that teaches problem-solving, planning and calming down through interactive activities, this is useful for younger students with oppositional tendencies.
- **Calm Counter.** This is a visual and audio app designed to help students recognise their feelings and learn coping skills to calm down.
- **Headspace.** This provides mindfulness and meditation sessions tailored for kids and teens.

Organisation and planning
- **MyHomework.** This is a planner that tracks assignments, tests and due dates. It improves time management.
- **Todoist.** A task-management app that helps students organise their homework and daily responsibilities, this allows them to break down tasks into manageable steps.
- **Trello.** A visual task board tool, this helps students with planning and organising tasks in a non-linear, flexible way that they control.

Communication

- **Avaz.** This is an augmentative and alternative communication (AAC) app designed to help students with speech challenges express their thoughts. It provides a range of customisable vocabulary and symbols, allowing students to communicate more effectively with teachers and peers.
- **Google Docs (with Voice Typing).** For older kids, Google Docs with the voice typing feature can reduce frustration related to written communication. Kids can express their thoughts more easily by speaking into the app, allowing their ideas to flow without the barrier of typing or handwriting.
- **Let's Be Social.** This focuses on teaching social and communication skills through stories and exercises that model appropriate responses in different social situations. Kids learn how to handle conversations, problem-solving and social interactions, which can be helpful for those with oppositional tendencies.
- **Speech Blubs.** A speech therapy app for younger students, this is particularly helpful for those with communication barriers. It uses interactive video modelling to help students practise pronunciation and sentence formation, building confidence in speaking.

Tools for conflict resolution and emotional expression

- **Emotionary.** An app that helps kids express emotions by selecting from a variety of illustrated feelings, this builds emotional vocabulary and helps students communicate their emotional state, fostering more productive conversations.
- **TalkingPoints.** A multilingual app that promotes communication between kids, teachers and families, this helps bridge language barriers and supports non-verbal kids by facilitating communication in different languages, including speech-to-text features.
- **Zones of Regulation.** This app is based on the Zones of Regulation framework and helps kids identify and express their emotions through colour-coded zones. By improving emotional awareness and communication, it supports better conflict resolution.

Virtual reality (VR) and augmented reality (AR)

- **CoSpaces Edu (AR/VR).** This allows kids to create their own virtual or augmented reality experiences. They can design immersive stories and social scenarios or even plan projects collaboratively in a shared virtual space. This not only promotes creativity but also helps students with communication, collaboration and organisation.
- **EmotiPlay (AR).** This is an augmented-reality-based platform designed to teach students emotional recognition and social interaction skills. Using AR, students can engage in role-playing activities that help them understand emotions, facial expressions and body language, improving their ability to navigate social situations. The platform provides interactive games and lessons where students can practise empathy, emotional regulation, and appropriate responses to social stimuli.
- **Floreo (VR).** This is a VR platform designed for individuals with autism, ADHD and social communication challenges. It offers immersive lessons on communication, social interactions and behavioural skills. Students can safely practise conversations, greetings and other social scenarios in a calm, controlled environment, helping them feel more confident and prepared in real-world interactions. The program includes lessons on calming techniques, navigating emotions, and handling social situations like maintaining personal space, making eye contact, and understanding emotions.
- **Mindshow (VR).** This is a VR tool that lets kids create their own animated stories, using avatars to act out scenes. This can help kids with defiance express their emotions in a non-threatening, creative way. Kids who may struggle to communicate verbally or face-to-face can use their avatars to practise conversation, problem-solving and social interactions. It allows for role-playing in a virtual world, encouraging emotional expression and creativity while practising communication skills.
- **Social Cipher (VR).** This is a game-based VR platform designed for neurodiverse students, particularly those who struggle with social cues and emotional regulation. Kids navigate a space adventure while engaging in conversations, making decisions, and managing conflicts.

The game helps them practise emotional regulation and problem-solving skills, which are essential for students with defiance. It encourages perspective-taking, empathy and emotional management in a non-threatening, gamified environment.
- **Unimersiv (VR).** This offers immersive educational experiences, helping kids focus on subjects like history, science and geography in a way that is engaging and interactive. For students with defiance who might struggle with traditional learning methods, VR can make learning more appealing and less confrontational, as they are more in control of the experience. It offers multisensory learning, which can be especially beneficial for neurodiverse students who respond well to visual and interactive environments.
- **Virtual Reality Social Cognition Training (VR-SCT).** This VR program is used to improve social cognition in students by placing them in various interactive social scenarios. Students can practise interpreting social cues, managing conversations, and responding appropriately to others' emotions. It is especially helpful for kids who might struggle with reading social cues or engaging in appropriate communication.

Parenting priorities for defiant kids

Big impacts
- parenting for collaboration – be a collaborator, not an enforcer
- have a good relationship with your child
- work with (rather than against) their teacher
- keep expectations high but lower demands
- social skills training.

Quick fixes
- working with your child rather than against them.

Waste of time
- feeling you should parent your child to meet the expectations of other adults
- 'toughening up'
- lots of rules and consequences

- punishment
- giving lectures about why something is really important
- pleading
- bargaining: 'If you do X, I'll do Y'.

If it's not one thing, it could also be another

There are some groupings of neurodiversity that can overlap in some kids. Kids can be on the spectrums and also have attention issues.

Similarities between defiance and the spectrums	
Strengths	<ul><li>Strong sense of justice</li><li>Honesty, especially in direct communication</li><li>Passionate about interest areas</li><li>Logical thinking</li><li>Creativity</li></ul>
Challenges	<ul><li>Difficulties complying with the demands of authorities</li><li>Conversation skills</li><li>Reading people accurately</li><li>Rigid thinking</li><li>Sensory sensitivities</li></ul>
Similarities between defiance and attention issues	
Strengths	<ul><li>Energy</li><li>Persistence</li><li>Passionate enthusiasts about interest areas</li><li>Strong sense of justice and fairness</li></ul>
Challenges	<ul><li>Impulsivity</li><li>Resistance to being told what to do</li><li>Poor concentration</li><li>Find it hard to calm themselves</li></ul>

Chapter 7

Movement and Coordination Issues or Dyspraxia

The gifts of movement issues or dyspraxia are creativity, kindness and perseverance. In the long term these gifts set people up for success in careers like medicine and health care, business administration, technology, creative arts and media production.

Young children learn initially though their senses and bodies. Issues to do with motor skills can include instability, low muscle tone, and imprecise movements that do not become more precise with practice or time.

Most people don't have to think much about their physical movements – they think about making an action and, hey presto, it happens! This is not the case for everyone.

Some neurodivergent kids find it challenging to complete tasks that require coordinated movements, such as writing, tying shoelaces or participating in sports. This is known as dyspraxia. These challenges go beyond the ability to learn new motor skills to the ability to learn a broader range of skills.

These kids have difficulty with coordinating the steps in some physical actions, from tying shoelaces to completing school assignments. Others might put their shoes on the wrong feet, struggle to tie up shoelaces, or put their clothes on backwards.

Struggling to coordinate smooth physical movements is also related to social challenges, planning and organisation skills, and time management.

The gifts of dyspraxia or movement issues set kids up for being adaptable and having determination when learning new ways and skills.

Discovering the neuroadvantages of movement issues

The brain patterns of children with movement issues commonly include variations in the functioning of:

- the cerebellum, which is involved in coordinating movement, balance and fine motor skills
- the corpus callosum, which connects the left and right sides of our brains, and may not communicate messages from one side to the other as well as in neurotypical children
- the parietal lobe, which plays a key role in spatial awareness, movement, planning, and the integration of sensory information, and may not function as effectively as in neurotypical children
- the basal ganglia, which are involved in motor control.

Primitive reflexes

In addition to having brain pathways that function differently, another contributing factor for children with movement challenges can be the presence of primitive reflexes.

We are all born with a series of primitive reflexes that help us to survive. As we mature, these primitive reflexes are inhibited and replaced by other physical movements. This usually occurs by three years of age, but not all children achieve this by that age. This can cause problems with muscle tone, balance and coordination that can delay learning.

The continued presence of primitive reflexes is associated with learning difficulties and may be seen in kids with dyspraxia, dyslexia, ADHD and the spectrums. The presence of some primitive reflexes has been found in 45 per cent of Year 5 and 6 students.

Three particular primitive reflexes to be aware of are:

1. the archer reflex, also known as the asymmetrical tonic neck reflex (ATNR)
2. the crawling or symmetrical tonic neck reflex (STNR)
3. the body curl and relax reflex or tonic labyrinthine reflex (TLR).

The archer reflex or the asymmetrical tonic neck reflex (ATNR)

This reflex is seen in most babies. When they move their head to one side, the arm on that side reaches out while the other arm is bent upwards (like an archer).

School-age children with this reflex will often place their books on an angle when writing. Some are seen as clumsy, accident-prone or inattentive.

This reflex can interfere with focusing visually, eye tracking, balance, skipping, sports, dancing and activities that involve crossing the midline of the body.

The crawling reflex or the symmetrical tonic neck reflex (STNR)

We all used this reflex as we started to crawl. A crawling child firstly looks up, then extends her neck, straightens her arms, bends her legs, and lowers her bottom as she sits on her heels.

As we get older, most of us inhibit this reflex and begin to walk. Children who have not inhibited this reflex often slump in their chairs, sit in a 'W' shape on the floor, find it difficult to catch a ball and may not be able to sit still when looking at the board at school.

Other kids slump over and write as if they were really short-sighted, even though their vision is normal.

The body curl and relax reflex or the tonic labyrinthine reflex (TLR)

When babies are on their back, they curl up if their head is moved towards their chest and extend their limbs if their head is lowered backwards. This natural reflex is usually inhibited by about six months of age.

Children who retain this reflex often have poor muscle tone and spatial reasoning challenges. They may also have difficulties with balance.

Signs that may indicate that primitive reflexes have not yet been inhibited

Can't sit straight

Some kids sit asymmetrically in chairs and can appear to some teachers to be inattentive or disrespectful. This can indicate the presence of a retained archer reflex or ATNR, as when one side of the body stretches out, the other side contracts.

Slump over while writing

The archer reflex or ATNR can also affect writing posture. These kids often slump over their writing, because stretching out one arm causes the other to flex. Stabilisation of the paper, and their grip on a pen or pencil, can also be affected. Another common reason that children slump while writing is poor eyesight, so I suggest they have their vision checked.

Lose track of their place when reading

Reading involves quick and smooth movements of the eyes. Some kids are unable to dissociate eye movement from head movement to localise, scan, track and shift their gaze. The student may lose their place and have difficulty locating letters, words or sentences on a page. This will also affect keyboard use and learning mathematics.

Poor ability to run

Often students with a retained archer reflex or ATNR have awkward running patterns, as they find it challenging to swing their arms reciprocally.

Splay when sitting on the floor

Students who sit on the floor in a 'W' shape (resting on their knees with their legs splayed behind them) may have retained their crawling reflex or STNR.

Floppy muscle tone

Undeveloped muscle tone and strength can also indicate retained crawling reflex or STNR. These kids may walk on their toes rather than on the soles of their feet. Others may be more likely to fall out of their seats than their peers.

Due to low levels of strength and tone, these kids often prefer to lie on the floor, have trouble learning to swim and are uncoordinated.

Poor impulse control

A retained crawling reflex or STNR can affect concentration. Some students find the pressure of the seat on their backs to be painful and may squirm and fidget to avoid this.

Inhibiting primitive reflexes

With special exercises for a few minutes each day over the course of six weeks, these primitive reflexes are inhibited and replaced by more usual actions.

While referral to a physical specialist may be advisable, parents and teachers can use these indicators to assess whether a referral is warranted. Parents and teachers can also help develop physical skills that promote learning by implementing a program such as 'Integrating Thinking', available at integratingthinking.com.au.

For a comprehensive description of primitive reflexes, see *Neuromotor Immaturity in Children and Adults: The INPP Screening Test for Clinicians and Health Practitioners* (Goddard Blythe, 2014) and toolstogrowot.com.

How parents can help

Despite their challenges, kids with movement issues or dyspraxia often possess unique strengths that can be leveraged in school, at work and in life.

As you will see later in this chapter, several new gizmos and methods exist that assist these kids to overcome challenges and to be successful.

Developing movement skills not only helps kids feel less awkward and clumsy, but it also helps with writing, sports or playing a musical instrument.

Step 1: Find their learning strengths

We create success for our children when we start from what is strong.

Use your child's top two learning strengths and combine this knowledge with the information below to start building their neuroadvantage.

Neuroadvantages of kids with movement issues

Planning and sequencing
- ✓ Visual steps in planning

Thinking and logic
- ✓ Careful analysis
- ✓ Logical problem-solving
- ✓ Methodical

Concentration and memory
- ✓ Structure steps of a task
- ✓ Good verbal memory

People smarts
- ✓ Kind
- ✓ Empathic
- ✓ Astute readers of social situations

Movement issues

Perceptual-motor skills
- ✓ Use of large muscle groups
- ✓ Flexibility

Language and word smarts
- ✓ Articulate
- ✓ Expressive

Spatial reasoning
- ✓ Design
- ✓ Art
- ✓ Lego sculpture
- ✓ Pattern detection and prediction

Number smarts
- ✓ Recall of patterns and sequences

© Andrew Fuller, *Neuroadvantage: The Strengths-based Approach to Neurodivergence* (Amba Press, 2025)

Step 2: Build on their learning strengths

Spatial reasoning

These children's ability to recall and solve problems using patterns, shapes and images is often remarkable. Interpreting charts, maps and visual depictions of data is an area of strength. They also often have abilities in predicting what comes next in a pattern, which applies to coding and to geometry.

Many of these kids almost compensate for their physical challenges by developing learning strengths in visual-spatial skills, which enable them to excel in tasks that involve visual reasoning, design and spatial awareness. Spatial reasoning helps to develop organisational skills.

We can develop these strengths further by playing games involving non-verbal problem-solving puzzles, blocks and jigsaws.

Perceptual-motor skills

While this is rarely an area of initial learning strength, parents can help children develop physical movements and perceptual-motor skills together.

Stress balls, therapy putty and games that enhance dexterity and coordination are helpful, such as counting steps while balancing.

Break down complex physical tasks (such as throwing and catching a ball) into smaller, teachable parts. For example:

1. Teach the stance.
2. Practise holding the ball.
3. Gradually work up to the full motion.

For some kids, there is an interesting overlap between movement issues and being double-jointed. Hyper-mobility of joints can increase movement difficulties.

We can strengthen this area through activities such as balance boards, standing on one foot for short periods, and yoga positions that improve posture and balance. Playing a musical instrument, dancing, catching-and-throwing games, games where players move from one 'stepping stone' on a floor to another, Twister, tapping and clapping, and even drum circles can all be helpful.

Activities like swimming, cycling and running also help improve physical coordination.

Concentration and memory

These kids often have strong memory skills and show high levels of perseverance with activities they are interested in. Giving structured step-by-step instructions and then minimising distractions assists their concentration.

Their recall of verbal information can help them in debates, creating stories and linking ideas.

Their awareness of patterns helps them to spot differences and discrepancies in information.

We can build on this learning strength by using audio stories, podcasts and storytelling.

Planning and sequencing

Planning is essentially intentionality. Sequencing is working out the steps to achieve an outcome you seek. These kids often solve problems in unique ways. We can help them to further their strengths by using visual checklists and flowcharts that break tasks down into steps, encouraging them to express each step verbally.

Using pre-written sticky notes can help to remind them of steps in daily routines. Activities like cooking, baking and gardening can help them to develop this learning strength further.

Thinking and logic

Kids with this learning strength often possess strong verbal skills, creative thinking and problem-solving abilities. They are often able to undertake careful analysis and have attention to detail. This enables them to develop a high level of analytical thinking.

This can be strengthened using logical puzzles that don't require fine motor skills, such as strategy games, chess, card games and riddles. Jigsaw puzzles or tangram sets encourage problem-solving and spatial reasoning. Scratch and Python can introduce these kids to coding, and STEM activities at school can give them an area of interest and success.

People smarts

These kids are often kind and show strong empathy and emotional sensitivity. Their own struggles in coordinating their movements often help them to appreciate the challenges faced by other people. They are often good listeners who are able to take on different perspectives and are attuned to social dynamics.

Arrange playdates or group activities where the child's strengths can shine, such as storytelling and creative games. You can develop this learning strength further by involving them in collaborative projects where their verbal and creative abilities are valued.

Language and word smarts

Kids with movement issues and learning strengths in language and words often develop strong verbal communication skills, which can compensate for their difficulties with written expression or motor tasks. They can be exquisitely articulate, possess a wicked sense of humour and have a considerable vocabulary. As a result, they can create compelling stories and also engage in critical thinking and persuasive pieces at a high level.

We can extend this learning strength by encouraging them to engage in analysis of texts, to consider the perspective of different characters and to write on themes of social equality and justice. Some will be attracted by debates, oral storytelling and drama.

Number smarts

Numbers can be relief for these kids, who can think about numbers in straightforward ways and use their analytical clarity to solve mathematical problems. Their pattern-detection skills set them up well to understand algebra and the relationships between numbers. Their analytical skills often enable them to detect trends in data and make accurate interpretations.

They can be better at explaining their mathematical reasoning verbally rather than writing it down.

We can extend this learning strength by helping them use calculators, mathematics apps and graphing and geometry software programs such as GeoGebra.

Leveraging their strengths with gizmos, tech and methods

Learning

Our mirror neurons are situated in the rear part of the prefrontal cortex. These activate when we watch other people doing intentional activities and help us to learn through imitation and role-modelling. Some of our most important learning happens through imitation after we watch successful people in action.

Some methods of improving inputs in this learning area include:

- balance and movement practice
- yoga
- dancing
- aerobics
- listening skills training
- origami
- constructing paper planes
- playing with and building Lego kits
- table tennis
- clapping and rhythm games
- rock climbing.

Simple animal-themed yoga poses (for example, cat-cow, downward dog) are helpful, as are stretching games that involve touching toes or reaching high points on a wall.

Use adaptive tools such as ergonomic pens, weighted utensils, or grips to improve control.

- **Dexteria.** An app designed to improve fine motor skills, Dexteria offers a range of exercises that focus on finger strength, coordination and dexterity. It's particularly useful for kids with dyspraxia who need to practise fine motor control.
- **FitMi Home Therapy.** This is a home therapy device that provides exercises to improve strength, balance and coordination. It's designed for people with motor difficulties and can be customised to target specific areas where students with dyspraxia may need help.
- Speech-to-text bypasses issues with writing and coordination.

- **Handwriting Without Tears.** This program offers a range of tools and apps to help students improve their handwriting skills. It provides exercises that break down the writing process into manageable steps, making it easier for kids with dyspraxia to practise.

Calming

Swimming, dancing and music are helpful.

Games like Wii Sports or Just Dance encourage full-body movement.

Apps focused on hand-eye coordination and reaction times are also useful.

Organisation and planning

- **GoNoodle.** This platform provides movement and mindfulness videos designed to get kids moving. It's particularly useful for students with dyspraxia who need to develop gross motor skills and improve coordination through fun, engaging activities.
- **OT Tools.** Many occupational therapy tools, such as weighted pens, pencil grips and slant boards, can be used in conjunction with apps to help kids with dyspraxia improve their writing skills. These tools are often recommended by occupational therapists and can make a significant difference in a student's ability to write comfortably and legibly.
- **Todoist.** A task-management app that helps students break down assignments into smaller, manageable tasks, this is particularly helpful for students with dyspraxia who may struggle with organising and prioritising their work.

Communication

Teach typing early, using programs like TypingClub or BBC Dance Mat Typing to build this skill.

As written communication can be a challenge for some of these kids, tools like Dragon NaturallySpeaking or built-in speech recognition in devices can reduce frustration in written communication.

- **Dragon NaturallySpeaking.** A powerful speech-to-text program that allows students to dictate their thoughts and have them converted into written text, this can be especially useful for students with dyspraxia who struggle with the physical act of writing.

- **Google Voice Typing.** This is a free, built-in speech-to-text tool available in Google Docs. It allows students to dictate their writing, helping them bypass the challenges of handwriting or typing.
- **Inspiration Maps.** A mind-mapping tool that helps kids visually organise their thoughts and ideas before writing, this can be especially helpful for students with dyspraxia who need to break down complex tasks into smaller, more manageable parts.

As the child grows, focus on building practical skills that align with their strengths, such as public speaking (leveraging verbal skills) or using advanced assistive technologies.

Parenting priorities for kids with movement issues

Big impacts

- highlighting and building on their strengths
- active learning
- structured routines
- motor skills development
- fun, engaging activities like tracing, drawing or mazes to reinforce fine motor skills
- weight-bearing activities or resistance bands to improve muscle tone and stability
- occupational therapy sessions tailored to improve fine motor skills (handwriting, cutting with scissors) and gross motor skills (balance, coordination).

Quick fixes

- providing visual or written checklists to help with task sequencing
- breaking tasks down into smaller chunks
- using large muscle groups
- weight training
- engaging in sports or physical activities that emphasise participation and fun rather than competition (swimming, yoga, martial arts)
- providing coaching or peer support to help with social interactions during activities

- encouraging activities like music (such as playing instruments with simple fingering), art or storytelling to highlight strengths and minimise motor demands.

Waste of time

- forcing these children into sports, activities or the playing of musical instruments that are beyond their physical movement skills.

If it's not one thing, it could also be another

Kids with movement issues often have poor coordination and difficulty acquiring motor skills. Movement issues and dyspraxia rarely occur in isolation. Movement issues are commonly seen in kids who also are on the spectrums. Attention issues and ADHD involve excessive movement and restlessness. Tourette's has sudden repetitive movements. This suggests overlapping pathways in the brain related to movement.

Similarities between movement issues and anxiety	
Strengths	<ul><li>Kindness and sensitivity to the feelings of others</li><li>Attention to detail</li><li>Persistence</li></ul>
Challenges	<ul><li>Wanting to avoid stressful or new situations</li><li>Tasks involving dexterity are challenging</li><li>Tendency to give up or avoid</li><li>Feeling embarrassed</li><li>Low self-esteem</li></ul>
Similarities between movement issues and the spectrums	
Strengths	<ul><li>Attention to detail</li><li>Strong visual memory and spatial reasoning</li><li>Strong focus in areas of interests</li><li>Logical thinking</li><li>Creative thinking</li></ul>
Challenges	<ul><li>Motor skills and coordination</li><li>Social communication</li><li>Anxiety</li></ul>

Similarities between movement issues and attention issues	
Strengths	<ul><li>Creative thinking</li><li>Emotional awareness</li><li>Planning and sequencing</li><li>Sensory sensitivities</li><li>Social skills</li></ul>
Challenges	<ul><li>Poor motor coordination</li><li>Tiredness</li><li>Organisational skills</li><li>Anxiety</li><li>Handwriting and fine motor tasks</li></ul>
Similarities between movement issues and sensory processing	
Strengths	<ul><li>Creative problem-solving</li><li>Kind, empathic people skills</li><li>Patterned recognition, especially of visual information</li></ul>
Challenges	<ul><li>Sensory overload and tiredness</li><li>Physical coordination and focus</li><li>Maintaining friendships</li></ul>
Similarities between movement issues and defiance	
Strengths	<ul><li>Justice and fairness</li><li>Persistence and determination</li><li>Directness</li><li>Creativity</li><li>Kindness</li></ul>
Challenges	<ul><li>Resistance to being told what to do</li><li>Motor coordination</li><li>Organisation and sequencing</li><li>Frustration tolerance</li><li>Collaborative problem-solving</li></ul>

Chapter 8

Reading Issues or Dyslexia

The gift of dyslexia is having direct experience of the world without too much influence of words, explanations and reasons. While many people hardly give themselves time to perceive anything before hurtling into a world of categories and words, kids with dyslexia remain largely free of these filters.

This sets them up to have more direct experiences which can convert into richer story creation, imaginative thinking and creativity, and an entrepreneurial can-do spirit.

In the long term, these gifts are seen as desirable in careers like sport, sales and marketing, STEAM careers (science, technology, engineering, art and mathematics), and entrepreneurial business.

Dyslexia makes it challenging to connect the sounds with the letters that make up words in reading and writing. Up to 17 per cent of school students have dyslexia. It seems to run in families, so probably has a genetic basis and relates to the ability to process the visual and auditory inputs into the brain.

To compensate for the underactivation in typical reading areas, kids with dyslexia may show overactivation in other brain regions, such as the spatial and visual areas or the frontal cortex. These areas are less efficient at processing reading tasks, leading to slower reading.

Dyslexia is often associated with difficulties in integrating visual and auditory information. For example, individuals with dyslexia may struggle to connect the visual representation of a letter with its corresponding sound.

Discovering the neuroadvantages of dyslexia

The brain patterns of children with dyslexia commonly include:

- disruptions in information pathways between the four main areas – Broca's area, the angular gyrus, the primary auditory cortex and Wernicke's area – which enable reading to occur easily
- underactivation in critical areas of the brain involved in reading and language processing.

Some research has suggested that individuals with dyslexia may have deficits in the magnocellular pathway, a visual processing pathway that is important for detecting motion and processing visual information quickly. This deficit could contribute to difficulties in tracking words and letters on a page.

How parents can help

As schools are so full of reading and words, it is all too easy for students with dyslexia to label themselves as 'dumb' or 'stupid'. It is our job to make sure they do not fall into the trap of believing this.

Step 1: Find their learning strengths

Go to www.mylearningstrengths.com to discover your child's learning strengths.

Step 2: Build on their learning strengths

We create success for our children when we start from what is strong.

Use your child's top two learning strengths and combine this knowledge with the information below to start building their neuroadvantage.

Many new gizmos and methods exist that help kids with dyslexia to overcome learning challenges and to be successful.

Spatial reasoning

Kids with dyslexia have strong spatial reasoning skills, which involve understanding and remembering the spatial relationships between objects.

Spatial reasoning can involve visualising objects in three dimensions and navigating complex environments. These skills are particularly useful

Neuroadvantages of kids with dyslexia

Planning and sequencing
✓ Sequential problem-solving skills

Thinking and logic
✓ Make connections others miss
✓ Logical sequences
✓ Creative problem-solving

Concentration and memory
✓ Visual memory

People smarts
✓ Strong sense of relatedness

Dyslexia

Perceptual-motor skills
✓ Often skilled at sports, dance crafts

Language and word smarts
✓ Verbal communication

Spatial reasoning
✓ Design
✓ Art
✓ Creative layouts
✓ Mechanical memory

Number smarts
✓ Good skills with numbers
✓ Hands-on learning
✓ Good with real-world problems

© Andrew Fuller, *Neuroadvantage: The Strengths-based Approach to Neurodivergence* (Amba Press, 2025)

in fields like architecture, engineering, set design, acting and visual arts. They can also be skilled in music, drawing, building and navigating. We can extend this learning strength by giving them hands-on activities.

Perceptual-motor skills

Kids with dyslexia can be very skilful at sports and construction. They often direct their energies and interests away from the world of words and reading towards doing things.

These kids are often good at sport and dance, where they are often adept at coordinating the movement of their bodies and integrating timing and rhythm. In the area of practical tasks, they are often skilled at crafts, woodwork, construction and carpentry.

We can expand on this learning strength by involving them in sports, construction, mechanics, drama, art or martial arts.

Concentration and memory

Kids with dyslexia may rely more on visual memory than on verbal memory, leading to strengths in tasks that require remembering and working with visual information. They often are able to recall and manipulate visual information effectively. This can be particularly advantageous in visual arts, design and any field that involves spatial or visual tasks.

Planning and sequencing

These kids have strong problem-solving skills, as they find alternative ways to process information and overcome challenges related to reading and writing. Once they are clear on the objective or outcome (often best presented visually), they can use their flexible thinking and adaptability to come up with innovative ways to achieve results.

If circumstances change, they are often able to think quickly and modify existing plans swiftly. They are often valued member of teams due to their strategic and flexible thinking.

Thinking and logic

Many individuals with dyslexia display enhanced creativity and the ability to think outside the box. They excel in generating novel ideas and approaches. They often excel in holistic thinking, meaning they can see the big picture and connect ideas across different domains.

This enables them to make connections between disparate ideas and see overarching patterns that others might miss. It also gives them the capacity to consider innovative approaches that others might miss and to change course quickly if circumstances change. This type of thinking is beneficial in fields that require strategic planning, innovation and systems thinking.

People smarts

These kids are willing to take risks, are persistent and are able to innovate. They often connect well with others, understand their needs and build strong relationships. This can be particularly beneficial in roles that require teamwork, leadership and communication.

They can have strong empathy and interpersonal skills, possibly as a result of their experiences with overcoming challenges and connecting with others.

Language and word smarts

These kids often have developed strengths in verbal reasoning (which involves understanding and analysing information presented verbally) and oral communication.

Number smarts

As long as mathematical problems are presented using symbols or real-world hands-on experiences (for example, blocks, dice, measurement of area), they can develop strong number smarts. Pure mathematical calculations can be an area of strength, but if problems are presented in ways that require a lot of complex reading, they often will avoid this area.

Kids with this learning strength are often able to visualise mathematical problems and combine these with their strengths in spatial reasoning (they often excel in trigonometry and algebra). Their big-picture thinking also gives them an advantage in financial literacy, measurement, and engineering design and calculations.

Leveraging their strengths with gizmos, tech and methods

Learning

- **Bookshare.** This is an online library of accessible eBooks for people with print disabilities, including dyslexia. The books can be read aloud using text-to-speech or braille, and the service includes a wide range of educational materials.
- **Ghotit Real Writer.** A writing and reading assistant specifically designed for people with dyslexia, this includes advanced spelling and grammar correction, word prediction, and text-to-speech to help students write more accurately and confidently.
- **Grammarly.** A writing assistant that helps with spelling, grammar and punctuation, this also provides suggestions for improving clarity and style, which can be helpful for students with dyslexia who struggle with written language.
- **Ginger.** Similar to Grammarly, Ginger offers spelling and grammar correction, but it also includes text-to-speech and translation features. It's designed to help users with dyslexia write more confidently.
- **Khan Academy.** This is an educational platform offering video lessons and interactive exercises across various subjects. The visual and auditory components of Khan Academy can help students with dyslexia better understand and retain information.
- **Kurzweil 3000.** An assistive technology tool that provides reading, writing and study support, this includes text-to-speech, dictionaries and tools for highlighting and taking notes. It's designed to help students with dyslexia better access and comprehend text.
- **Learning Ally.** This is an audiobook service that provides access to thousands of audiobooks, including textbooks and literature. The audiobooks are read by human narrators, which can be particularly helpful for students who struggle with text-based reading.
- **Prizmo.** A scanning and OCR (optical character recognition) app, this allows students to take pictures of text and have it read aloud. It's useful for reading books, worksheets and other printed materials.
- **Quizlet.** This is a study app that allows students to create flashcards, take practice quizzes and engage in interactive learning games.

It's particularly helpful for memorising facts and vocabulary, which can be challenging for students with dyslexia.
- **Read&Write.** A literacy support toolbar that integrates with web browsers and Microsoft Office, this offers text-to-speech, word prediction, dictionaries and highlighting tools, making it easier for students with dyslexia to read, write and study.
- **Touch-type Read and Spell (TTRS).** This is a typing program that teaches touch-typing while reinforcing reading and spelling skills. It's especially beneficial for students with dyslexia, as it uses a multi-sensory approach to learning.

Organisation and planning

- **Evernote.** This is a versatile app for organising notes, to-do lists and ideas. Kids can add images, voice recordings and handwritten notes, making it easier to capture and organise information.
- **Inspiration Maps.** A mind-mapping and outlining tool that helps kids visually organise their thoughts and ideas, this is particularly useful for planning essays and projects, as it allows for a visual representation of information.
- **Kidspiration Maps.** A mind-mapping app designed for younger kids, this allows children to create visual representations of their ideas and thoughts, making it easier to understand and retain information.
- **Microsoft OneNote.** This is a note-taking app that allows kids to organise their notes, add images and record audio.
- **MindMeister.** A mind-mapping tool that helps kids visually organise their thoughts and ideas, this is useful for brainstorming, planning essays and studying complex subjects.
- **Notability.** This app combines note-taking, sketching and PDF annotation. It supports handwriting, typing, audio recordings and importing PDFs, making it a powerful tool for students with dyslexia to keep their notes organised and accessible.
- **Popplet.** A visual organising app that allows kids to create mind maps and diagrams, this is an excellent tool for visual learners who need to see the connections between ideas.

Communication

- **ClaroSpeak.** This is a text-to-speech app with word prediction, speech recognition and spell-checking features. It's particularly helpful for kids who need assistance with writing and editing their work.
- **Co:Writer.** A word-prediction app that helps kids with dyslexia write more efficiently by suggesting words as they type, this also includes speech recognition and text-to-speech features, which assist with writing and reading back what's been written.
- **Dragon NaturallySpeaking.** This is a powerful speech-to-text program that allows kids to dictate their thoughts and have them converted into written text. It's particularly useful for students with dyslexia who struggle with writing.
- **Google Voice Typing.** A free speech-to-text tool available in Google Docs, this allows kids to dictate their writing, which can help bypass some of the challenges associated with typing or writing by hand.
- **NaturalReader.** This is a text-to-speech app that converts written text into spoken words, helping students with dyslexia read more easily. It supports various file formats, including PDFs, Word documents and web pages.
- **Simplex Spelling.** A phonics-based spelling app that teaches students how to spell using phonetic patterns, this is designed to improve spelling skills through practice and reinforcement of phonics rules.

Parenting priorities for kids with dyslexia

Big impacts

- creative projects
- building on their learning strengths
- building a family that has good communication strategies and ways of checking if misunderstandings occur
- Omega-3 (fish oil or flaxseed oil)
- technology.

Quick fixes

- using tech gizmos that overcome the barriers to learning, such as speech-to-text software
- physical games and sports to calm them.

Waste of time
- telling them to focus or work harder.

If it's not one thing, it could also be another

There are some groupings of neurodiversity that can overlap in some kids.

Similarities between dyslexia and anxiety	
Strengths	• Sensitivity and kindness • Creativity • Hands-on visual learning • Attention to detail in learning strengths
Challenges	• Refusal to read • Fear of failure and avoidance • Low confidence • Slow processing of complex information
Similarities between dyslexia and the spectrums	
Strengths	• Passionate interests • Engrossed and enthusiastic about key interest areas • Can think deeply and logically • Spatial reasoning – thinking in pictures • Creative thinking
Challenges	• Making and keeping friends • Sustaining attention • Restless and distractible • Understanding metaphors and imagery in literature • Reading • Slower information processing (require more time)
Similarities between dyslexia and attention issues	
Strengths	• Creative problem-solving • Verbal communication skills • Preference for active, hands-on learning experiences • Entrepreneurialism

Challenges	• Usually have some executive functions that require development (see Part 2 of this book) • High interrelationship between dyslexia and attention issues in 25–40 per cent of cases • Struggle in 'word-rich' school classrooms • Unwillingness to read • Managing frustrations

Similarities between dyslexia and sensory sensitivities

Strengths	• Big-picture thinkers and creative problem-solvers • Spatial reasoning and visualisation skills • Emotional awareness and people skills
Challenges	• Challenges in written language • Sensory overload • Slower to process information

Similarities between dyslexia and defiance

Strengths	• Justice and fairness • Persistence and determination • Directness • Hands-on learning
Challenges	• Don't like being told what to do • Reading • Calming

Similarities between dyslexia and movement issues

Strengths	• Creative problem-solving • Use of language and words when writing is not involved • Empathy and kindness • Persistence
Challenges	• Reading and language • Organisation and sequencing • Slow processing, especially of written tasks • Fine and gross motor skills • Low confidence

Chapter 9

Mathematics Issues or Dyscalculia

One of the main gifts of dyscalculia and not having a head for numbers is intuitive and creative thinking. When away from numbers, these kids think astutely in verbal and visual ways.

In the long term these gifts give people an advantage in careers like creative arts, practical sciences, environmental and landscape management, defence, justice and law enforcement, and skilled trades that do not require complex mathematical calculations.

If you have ever struggled to get your head around numbers, this may resonate with you. However, dyscalculia goes well beyond just having a bit of a struggle with using numbers – heads swim, brains go foggy, minds go blank, and kids break out into a cold sweat.

Kids with dyscalculia look at numbers anxiously as if they were mysterious hieroglyphs and they lack the Rosetta Stone.

These kids are as smart as they need to be, but their processing of numbers is a monumental struggle.

Kids with dyscalculia often have trouble retrieving basic arithmetic facts from memory, such as addition and multiplication tables. Times tables slip out of their memory. Their number troubles don't just exist in classrooms; some have trouble reading the time, counting money, estimating distances and time, and keeping score in sports games.

This difficulty stems from impaired connections between the brain regions responsible for storing and accessing numerical knowledge.

The gifts of kids with dyscalculia set them up for success in careers that value intuition and human connection over technical calculations such as design, writing, counselling and some areas of teaching.

Discovering the neuroadvantages of dyscalculia

The brain patterns of children with dyscalculia commonly include the following variations:

- The parts of the brain that process numbers don't function in the usual ways. The intraparietal sulci of the parietal lobe, which are critical for number processing and arithmetic tasks, function differently. This part of the brain also processes rhythm, movement and music, which suggests an interesting overlap between music and mathematical processing. (Thus Pythagoras, who is well known for mathematics, was also the first person credited with identifying the octave in music.) However, as with much research in neurodivergence, the relationship between music and mathematical processing is not straightforward. Neurodivergent kids remain resolutely individual. While some may possess skills in both music and mathematics, others may have great capacity in one area but not in the other. Of course, this underscores the importance of knowing each child's pattern of learning strengths.
- When confronted by numbers, the amygdala (fear centre) activates, and the hippocampus (conscious memory) is restricted by cortisol.
- Some studies suggest that the occipital lobe, which is involved in visual processing, may also be implicated in dyscalculia.

How parents can help

You may never get your child to love numbers, but you can at least help them to survive in a world that relies on numbers. A future of uncompleted tax returns, unpaid bills and possibly soaring credit debt is worth avoiding for anyone.

Being unable to think in numbers may not only reduce school results; it may also increase the risk of being ripped off by others.

Neuroadvantages of kids with dyscalculia

Planning and sequencing
- ✓ Visual planning
- ✓ Checklists
- ✓ Storyboards

Thinking and logic
- ✓ Creative and artistic thinking
- ✓ Visual arts
- ✓ Systems thinking

Concentration and memory
- ✓ Good memory for non-numerical parts of maths problems
- ✓ Thinking of maths problems as being like a recipe

People smarts
- ✓ Collaboration
- ✓ Good team members
- ✓ Sensitive to others

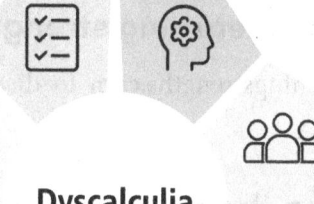

Dyscalculia

Perceptual-motor skills
- ✓ Rhythms in dance, sport and music

Language and word smarts
- ✓ Creative storytelling
- ✓ Communication

Spatial reasoning
- ✓ Visual reasoning
- ✓ Thinking in connections between shapes, sizes and colours

Number smarts
- ✓ Practical, real-world, hands-on applications of numbers

© Andrew Fuller, *Neuroadvantage: The Strengths-based Approach to Neurodivergence* (Amba Press, 2025)

Know that your kid is smart and their challenges are mainly to do with processing numbers. Using the areas in which they are smart to help them to think in numbers is the best way of improving the situation. These strategies are outlined below.

It doesn't matter how much practice they do; number concepts just don't click in the way they do for other people. Getting stressed about this, or insisting they do special mathematics practice or tutoring, or just try harder, doesn't work.

Dyscalculia runs in families.

Try to find ways to link thinking about numbers with your child's areas of interest, such as sports scores, saving up money, shopping, musical rhythms or designing a skate ramp.

Step 1: Find their learning strengths

Go to www.mylearningstrengths.com to discover your child's learning strengths.

Step 2: Build on their learning strengths

We create success for our children when we start from what is strong.

Use your child's top two learning strengths and combine this knowledge with the information below to start building their neuroadvantage.

Spatial reasoning

One of the most effective ways of teaching mathematical thinking is the Singapore bar method, which uses hands-on, visual ways of thinking about numbers. Many kids with dyscalculia possess strong visual and spatial reasoning skills, which enable them to understand and manipulate objects in space effectively. They are also capable of thinking in three dimensions, which can advantage them in activities like drawing, sculpture, surveying and navigating. There are many YouTube clips on the Singapore bar method, notably those featuring Dr Yeap Ban Har.

Perceptual-motor skills

These kids may struggle with numbers as an abstract concept and yet have a good understanding of times tables and percentages in sporting contexts. Others will find numbers meaningless, but if you ask them to pace out the length of a household block or work out the dimensions of an area of garden, they can be quite skilled.

They are often skilled at recognising rhythms and repeated patterns in music, dance or physical movement sequences.

They may also be skilled at visual-motor tasks like assembling puzzles or completing construction activities.

Concentration and memory

Some kids with dyscalculia are so stricken at the thought of having to think in numbers that they freeze up. Kids who otherwise have good concentration and memory levels can be overtaken by fear and cortisol. Cortisol not only makes it harder to focus; it also blocks our memory.

When away from the world of numbers, these kids have good levels of concentration and memory. They are often skilled at creative storytelling, pattern detection and focused thinking.

One way to help kids is to suggest that mathematics can be like cooking. It is like making a cake. You need ingredients and a method to reach an outcome. When baking a cake, your ingredients include eggs, flour, sugar and butter. Your method involves mixing the ingredients, baking and icing. In 'recipe' maths, you use the ingredients and follow the steps to reach the answer.

For example, if I am trying to find an average, my ingredients are the scores and the number of responses. The method is to add up all the scores and then divide the total by the number of responses.

Imagine spreading all of the ingredients in front of you. Ask yourself: What have I got in front of me? What am I supposed to create with them? In what different ways could I combine these ingredients?

This method is about reducing anxiety and providing structure to learning. Of course, this method can apply to cooking up answers to deeper questions about the universe too.

While some mathematics teachers will not like the idea of recipe maths, to pass basic mathematics in school doesn't always require a deep understanding. Knowing what ingredients go in what order to create the outcome needed can be sufficient.

Planning and sequencing

There is a risk that, without planning skills, these kids will make wildly hopeful guesses rather than develop strategies that they can apply to solve mathematical problems.

Kids with learning strengths in planning and sequencing may be able to incorporate numbers into their plans. For example, they could number the steps involved in an action plan or checklist.

They are often skilled at creating visual plans – such as storyboards, diagrams or visual organisers – to outline steps and processes. As they are used to finding ways to see thing from different perspectives, they are usually flexible in reordering steps or adapting plans based on new information.

Thinking and logic

Kids with dyscalculia often exhibit creativity and artistic talent in areas that do not directly involve numbers, such as music, visual arts or creative writing.

They often develop creative approaches to problem-solving, especially when traditional methods are challenging, and may find alternative ways to understand concepts and complete tasks. They are often able to understand how different components interact within a system.

Often able to draw logical conclusions from information given (deductive reasoning), they can be skilled problem-solvers.

People smarts

Many kids with dyscalculia develop good skills in collaboration. They are aware that other people possess skills that they don't possess. In a world that prizes numbers so highly, it is easy for these kids to dismiss their own smarts. Some will need to learn that they have skills that others do not possess. They often have good communication skills, are attentive listeners and are valued as team members.

Others may not love numbers but become interested when they think about how numbers relate to people they know. For example:

How many people out of ten have blue eyes?

How many people out of ten are left-handed?

Let's survey ten people we know and ask them to tell us their favourite number and why.

Language and word smarts

These kids are articulate expressers of language. They can reason verbally, read and comprehend clearly, and often develop well in areas like music, visual arts or creative writing.

Mathematics contains its own special language, and just like any new language it needs to be learned. Be consistent with the language used and try to relate mathematics to your kids' lives by using non-mathematical language to explain new ideas and concepts.

Asking them to tell you about a mathematical problem will often be helpful, as they can outline their reasoning better verbally than numerically.

Mathematical reasoning is thinking in numbers, and we can express many of the issues in language rather than numbers. This is well described in 'The Montessori Story of Numbers': www.themontessorischool.wa.edu.au/methodology/montessori-great-stories/the-montessori-story-of-numbers/.

Number smarts

Usually this is not a learning strength. Nevertheless, these kids can be quite adept at estimating costs during shopping, understanding time schedules, and following recipes.

Real-world numbers are fine; it is when mathematical ideas become abstract that they struggle.

The use of technology helps many of these young people to overcome barriers regarding numbers.

Leveraging their strengths with gizmos, tech and methods

Learning

- Real-life experiences: counting coins, planning a meal, following a recipe, buying groceries.
- Plan a trip: look at timetables, consider distances and times.
- Cut a cake or an apple into equal portions.
- The Singapore bar method.

- Tools like blocks, number lines, slices of pizza or cake, and visual charts can help make numbers more understandable.
- **The Dyscalculia Screener:** dyscalculiascreener.org
- **Dragonbox.** This offers a series of maths games that introduce algebraic concepts in a fun and engaging way. The games are designed to teach students the logic of maths through visual puzzles, making them particularly useful for kids who struggle with traditional maths instruction.
- **DysCalculator.** This is an app specifically designed for individuals with dyscalculia. It helps them understand numbers and arithmetic operations by providing both numerical and visual representations of calculations. Kids can input numbers and see the corresponding total in a visual format, aiding in number comprehension.
- **Elephant Learning Math Academy.** This app is designed to help with maths learning difficulties by focusing on foundational concepts. It uses adaptive learning to adjust the difficulty level based on the kid's progress, making it ideal for kids with dyscalculia who need personalised instruction.
- **Khan Academy Kids.** This app offers a wide range of educational activities, including maths games and exercises that help build foundational maths skills. It uses engaging characters and interactive tasks to make learning maths enjoyable for young children.
- **Modmath.** A maths app that helps kids with dyscalculia and dysgraphia, this provides a digital graph-paper interface where kids can complete maths problems without struggling with handwriting. The app supports basic arithmetic, fractions and more-complex algebraic equations.
- **Photomath.** This allows kids to take a picture of a maths problem and provides step-by-step solutions. The app is particularly helpful for kids with dyscalculia who struggle with understanding the process behind mathematical operations. It also offers visual explanations to help make abstract concepts more concrete. The more thinking in numbers is made real, the better. For example, use blocks, dice or card games to help kids think about quantities better.

Organisation and planning

- **MyStudyLife.** This is a planner app that helps kids organise their schoolwork and manage their time effectively. It's particularly useful for students with dyscalculia who may struggle with keeping track of assignments, test dates and study schedules.
- **Talking Calculator.** An app that reads out numbers and operations aloud as they are entered, this can help kids with dyscalculia verify their inputs and better understand the calculations they are performing.
- **Voice Dream Reader.** This is a text-to-speech app that can help kids with dyscalculia by reading maths problems and instructions aloud. This can reduce the cognitive load associated with processing text and allow students to focus on the mathematical concepts.

Parenting priorities for kids with dyscalculia

Big impacts

- start with areas of learning strength
- hands-on experiential mathematics activities – use diagrams, flowcharts and colour coding.

Quick fixes

- lowering anxiety and pressure
- real-world examples of numbers and how they link to areas of interest or learning strengths
- short bursts of thinking about numbers as they occur in everyday life – shopping, cooking, etc.

Waste of time

- telling these kids not to worry, as you had the same problem too
- increasing pressure
- focusing on getting the right answer (rather than developing understanding)
- rewards (or consequences) for completion or non-completion of mathematical problems.

If it's not one thing, it could also be another

Similarities between dyscalculia and the spectrums	
Strengths	<ul><li>Recognising patterns</li><li>Visual problem-solving</li><li>Systematic thinking</li></ul>
Challenges	<ul><li>Overloaded by too many numbers or complex problems</li><li>Abstract mathematics concepts</li><li>Fear of failure</li></ul>

Similarities between dyscalculia and attention issues	
Strengths	<ul><li>Creative thinking</li><li>Spatial reasoning</li><li>Hands-on learning</li></ul>
Challenges	<ul><li>Impulsive guessing at answers</li><li>Short concentration spans</li><li>Avoidance</li></ul>

Similarities between dyscalculia and sensory sensitivities	
Strengths	<ul><li>Sensitivity to blocks, shapes, textures, colours as a way of understanding numbers</li><li>Creative problem-solving</li></ul>
Challenges	<ul><li>Sense of being overwhelmed and avoiding numbers</li><li>Emotional regulation</li><li>Avoidance of thinking in numbers</li></ul>

Similarities between dyscalculia and defiance	
Strengths	<ul><li>Determination</li><li>Advocacy</li><li>Tendency to defy or ignore instructions</li></ul>
Challenges	<ul><li>Managing frustrations</li><li>Impulsivity and poor planning</li><li>Defiance can conceal fear of failure</li></ul>

Similarities between dyscalculia and movement issues	
Strengths	- Adaptability - Big-picture thinking - Conceptual discussion and strategy formulation
Challenges	- Movement limitations can interfere with hands-on application of mathematical concepts - Fine motor skills – tracing, mapping, using blocks and dice can be difficult - Lowered confidence
Similarities between dyscalculia and dyslexia	
Strengths	- Creative big-picture thinking - Spatial reasoning - Problem-solving
Challenges	- Processing numerical information and reading - Remembering sequences - Slow processing of information

Chapter 10

Drawing and Writing Issues or Dysgraphia

The gift of dysgraphia is the ability to think deeply and innovatively and express thoughts creatively. In the long term these gifts are highly valued in careers like communication and media, nature and outdoor careers, agriculture, business and entrepreneurship, performing arts and technology.

Getting thoughts out of their head and onto paper is a challenge for these kids. Despite being smart and having clarity of thinking, what ends up on the page looks like the indecipherable scribbles of a busy doctor. They usually have slow, effortful handwriting with irregular letter sizes, inconsistent spacing and poor alignment. Spelling is also often an issue.

Of course, in a world of speech-to-text technologies and spellcheckers, this may not be the barrier it once was.

Dysgraphia is linked to difficulties in the parts of the brain that coordinate motor planning and execution.

Discovering the neuroadvantages of drawing issues and dysgraphia

The brain patterns of children with dysgraphia commonly include variations in the functioning of:

- the parietal lobe (beneath the crown of the head), which integrates sensory information and helps to coordinate motor skills, which are crucial for writing

- Broca's area on the left side of the frontal lobes, which is related to language expression and motor planning (kids with dysgraphia may exhibit differences in the structure and function of this area, leading to difficulties in organising and producing written language)
- the prefrontal cortex, responsible for higher-order motor planning and thinking, which shows atypical activity in people with dysgraphia (this can create challenges in planning the sequence of movements required for writing, leading to slow, laborious handwriting or poorly formed letters)
- the cerebellum, at the bottom of the brain, which assists in motor control and coordination.

In addition, communication between the frontal and parietal lobes, involved in writing, may be less efficient in individuals with dysgraphia, leading to difficulties in integrating motor and linguistic processes.

How parents can help

These kids understand a lot more than they can express in writing, so never underestimate them.

When we grip pens or pencils to write or draw, we use the smaller muscles of the hand. These are our fine motor skills. Writing well involves coordinating our fine motor muscles, some being used to shift a pen or pencil up and down while others move it sideways. These are the same small muscles that we use for knitting, sewing, stitching, using scissors and cooking.

Kids who struggle with their writing or drawing may grip a pen or pencil oddly or write only in block writing, often pressing too hard on the page. Placing a rubberised mouse pad beneath their paper can help them to learn how much pressure to exert when writing. You can assist kids who display poor pen or pencil grip by marking the positions on their fingers where the pen or pencil should touch as they hold it.

Pencil grips, slant boards and keyboards can lessen tiredness and physical strain.

Some of these kids also lose track of where they are on a page as they write, because they look at their writing hand instead of the page. Helping them learn to write while looking away fixes this.

Neuroadvantages of kids with drawing issues or dysgraphia

Planning and sequencing
- ✓ Visual and physical ways of sequencing events and prioritisation

Thinking and logic
- ✓ Creative and analytical thinking

People smarts
- ✓ Listening skills
- ✓ Relationship skills
- ✓ Negotiation and persuasion skills

Concentration and memory
- ✓ Physical focus
- ✓ Rhythmic memory
- ✓ Spatial memory

Perceptual-motor skills
- ✓ Large muscle groups
- ✓ Tactile sensitivity
- ✓ Learning through movement

Dysgraphia

Language and word smarts
- ✓ Comprehension
- ✓ Analysis
- ✓ Rich vocabulary

Spatial reasoning
- ✓ Visual reasoning
- ✓ Design
- ✓ Pattern recognition

Number smarts
- ✓ Numerical reasoning
- ✓ Abstract conceptual thinking (geometry, algebra)

© Andrew Fuller, *Neuroadvantage: The Strengths-based Approach to Neurodivergence* (Amba Press, 2025)

Step 1: Find their learning strengths

Go to www.mylearningstrengths.com to discover your child's learning strengths.

Step 2: Build on their learning strengths

We create success for our children when we start from what is strong. Prepare your child for success by indicating, using arrows or borders, where they should write down words on a page.

Use your child's top two learning strengths and combine this knowledge with the information below to start building their neuroadvantage.

Spatial reasoning

Children's struggle to express their concepts in writing can mislead them into thinking that they are not good at thinking generally. This is not true.

Kids with challenges in writing and drawing often possess learning strengths in visual reasoning, design and spatial awareness. They are often adept at understanding and manipulating objects in space. These abilities are valuable in fields like art, architecture and engineering.

As you will see later, several new gizmos exist that help these kids to overcome challenges and to be successful. We can build on spatial reasoning as a learning strength with these kids by involving them in puzzles, mapping and geometry. Clay or 3D modelling and art also help. At school, they will often excel in STEAM subjects (science, technology, engineering, art and mathematics).

Perceptual-motor skills

While fine hand movements may not be their strongest area, they are often capable gymnasts, dancers and athletes, especially in sports involving large muscle groups, such as football, running and hurdles. Many will find playing the violin or piano to be tricky but may find success with drums or trombones.

As we refine a perceptual-motor skill, some aspects become automatic. Most of us are so accustomed to doing this, we don't think about it. After getting into a car, you don't have to think 'What do I do first?' If you pick up a pen, you don't have to consider, 'Now, how do I write, again?' These processes have been built through repetition over time, shifting from conscious thought to muscle memory.

When an action or movement is so well rehearsed or practised, like riding a bicycle or tying shoelaces, the memory of that movement is retained in the motor cortex, the basal ganglia and the cerebellum. It becomes an acquired skill that seems innate.

We can develop this learning strength further through physical learning that initially focuses on large muscle groups and then, as those skills are accomplished, develop fine motor aspects of the skills.

Concentration and memory

These kids can develop phenomenal memory skills, including memorising facts, sequences and verbal information. For these kids, concentration and memory are often strengthened through verbal repetition, finding the most important aspect of an idea, self-explanations ('First I've got to do … then I've got to do') and hands-on practice.

Generally, these kids have an excellent memory for sequences and patterns, especially when they are presented to them visually or verbally.

Planning and sequencing

Finding ways for these kids to visually plan will improve this learning strength even further. Coloured checklists, flowcharts, diagrams and illustrations that outline the steps towards completion of a goal help.

We can further build this learning strength by helping kids to learn to do 'step-through planning and problem-solving'. Asking them to take a step for each part of a plan, like someone using stepping stones to cross a river, helps them in planning, decision-making and problem-solving.

Thinking and logic

These kids often have strong creative, critical-thinking and problem-solving skills. They are often able to verbally or visually analyse an issue or problem. This is helpful in maths, science and logical reasoning.

Conversations that discuss the advantages and disadvantages of ideas or approaches are valuable.

This area can be further strengthened by helping them to become good probability thinkers and also being able to prioritise. You can also use the step-through approach described above to help them to think about what aspect of an issue or problem to be addressed is the highest priority, with the highest-priority issue being considered with the first step, down to the lowest-priority issue with the last step.

People smarts

These kids often develop kindness, strong empathy and interpersonal skills, which helps them build meaningful relationships. People with dysgraphia can be effective team members, particularly in environments that value diverse skills and perspectives.

Generally, they are good conversationalists who listen well, are socially aware and find a really solid group of friends.

Language and word smarts

These kids are skilled at creative expression that does not rely on writing in areas such as art, music or drama. Their verbal communication skills compensate for their difficulties with written expression.

They often possess a rich vocabulary and can use their strong analytical and comprehension skills to create compelling stories. Encourage them to be imaginative and vivid in their language and in conversations.

Number smarts

When working purely with numbers, these kids are fine. The clarity of just dealing with numbers without the addition of words benefits many of them. For this reason, we need to isolate numerical reasoning from worded problems. For example:

> *With problems like '3 + 2 = ?' they will be fine.*
>
> *With problems like 'If Johnny has three apples and Jenny has two apples, how many apples do both of them have?' they will struggle.*

These kids are good conceptual thinkers who can reason numerically and complete calculations in algebra and geometry.

Leveraging their strengths with gizmos, tech and methods

Learning

- Read to them. Read with them.
- Encourage them to do drawing and colouring in.
- Support their expression using language.
- Take them to acting classes.

- **Cogmed or Lumosity.** These programs can help improve working memory and attention.
- **Dragon NaturallySpeaking.** This speech-to-text program allows kids to dictate their thoughts and have them converted into written text.
- **Google Voice Typing.** This is a free, built-in speech-to-text tool available in Google Docs. It allows students to dictate their writing, helping them bypass handwriting or typing difficulties.
- **Modmath.** An app designed for kids with dysgraphia and dyslexia, this provides a digital graph-paper interface where students can type maths problems instead of writing them by hand. It helps with organisation and ensures that numbers and symbols are correctly aligned.
- **NaturalReader.** A text-to-speech tool that converts written text into spoken words, this helps kids with dysgraphia by allowing them to listen to text, which can reduce the cognitive load associated with reading and writing.
- **Voice Dream Writer.** This includes speech-to-text functionality along with text-to-speech feedback. It helps kids with dysgraphia to compose text using their voice and then hear it read back to them for proofreading.

Organisation and planning

- **Evernote.** A versatile note-taking app that helps kids organise their notes, to-do lists, and ideas, this allows for multimedia input, including text, images and audio, making it easier for kids with dysgraphia to capture and organise information.
- **Inspiration Maps.** A mind-mapping tool that helps kids visually organise their thoughts and ideas before writing, this can be especially helpful for kids with dysgraphia who need to break down complex tasks into smaller, more manageable parts.
- **MindMeister.** A mind-mapping app that helps kids organise their thoughts visually, this is ideal for planning essays, projects and other writing tasks that require clear structure and organisation.
- **MyHomework Student Planner.** This app helps kids track assignments, tests and other tasks. It's particularly useful for kids with dysgraphia who may struggle with organisation and time management.

- **Notability.** An app that combines handwriting, typing, audio recording and PDF annotation, this is particularly useful for kids who need to integrate multiple forms of input into their notes and written work.
- **OneNote.** A digital note-taking app that allows users to organise their notes, create to-do lists, and add images or audio recordings, this is particularly useful for kids who need to keep their work organised and accessible in a non-linear format.
- **Popplet.** This app allows kids to create visual diagrams and mind maps. It is useful for brainstorming and organising ideas, making it easier for kids to structure their writing.

Communication

Many speech-to-text apps are useful for these kids.

- **Grammarly.** This is an online writing assistant that checks for spelling, grammar and punctuation errors. It also offers suggestions for improving clarity and style, which can be helpful for kids with dysgraphia who struggle with writing mechanics.
- **Handwriting Without Tears.** This is a research-based program for teaching handwriting to children designed by occupational therapists.
- **Kurzweil 3000.** An assistive technology tool that provides reading, writing and study support, this includes text-to-speech, dictionaries and writing tools, making it easier for students with dysgraphia to access and produce written content.
- **Livescribe Smartpen.** This is a digital pen that records audio while you write. Kids can later replay the audio by tapping on their notes, which can help with reviewing and understanding written content.
- **TypingClub.** This is a typing tutor program that helps kids improve their keyboarding skills. Typing can often be a more accessible way for students with dysgraphia to produce written work.

Parenting priorities for kids with drawing issues and dysgraphia

Big impacts
- reading stories to them and with them
- helping them become expressive communicators in ways that don't rely on writing
- finding and building on strengths
- patient, calm parenting.

Quick fixes
- celebrate small advances in achievement
- low- or no-pressure family environments.

Waste of time
- overemphasising the importance of writing
- increasing pressure on kids to write.

If it's not one thing, it could also be another

	Similarities between the spectrums and dysgraphia
Strengths	<ul><li>Noticing patterns and details</li><li>Visual thinking</li><li>Analytical and logical reasoning skills</li></ul>
Challenges	<ul><li>Challenges with planning, sequencing, and organising tasks can make written assignments overwhelming</li><li>Sensory sensitivities such as tactile aversion to pencil grip or texture of paper</li><li>Frustration with writing tasks can trigger emotional outbursts or avoidance</li></ul>
	Similarities between attention issues and dysgraphia
Strengths	<ul><li>Divergent, creative thinking, generating innovative ideas and creative solutions with storytelling or visual arts</li><li>Seeing the big picture and conceptualising overarching ideas</li><li>Strong verbal skills, allowing them to articulate their thoughts and ideas effectively</li></ul>

Challenges	• Getting started – task initiation • Limited working memory, making it difficult to retain ideas and to follow multi-step instructions • Slow processing speed can make some tasks disproportionately time-consuming • Teach planning, time management and organisational strategies explicitly using visual aids like checklists or timers to guide task completion
Similarities between defiance and dysgraphia	
Strengths	• Out-of-the-box thinking and resourcefulness • Creative expression of ideas • High energy and determination • Sense of fairness and equity, which can be a powerful strength when guided constructively • Strong leadership skills when paired with emotional regulation strategies
Challenges	• Organising ideas on paper especially difficult, leading to frustration and avoidance • Managing emotions and frustration • Power struggles with teachers, if expectations are seen as rigid or unfair • Low self-esteem
Similarities between movement issues and dysgraphia	
Strengths	• Thinking in novel ways, offering unique perspectives in discussions and projects • Emotionally sensitive • Tend to focus on broader concepts rather than getting bogged down in details
Challenges	• Difficulties with gross motor skills (e.g., running, catching) and fine motor coordination (e.g., tying shoelaces, using scissors) • Both conditions often involve slower processing speed and difficulties holding and manipulating information, affecting problem-solving and time-bound tasks • Motor difficulties can make tasks physically exhausting, leading to frustration and disengagement

Similarities between dyscalculia and dysgraphia	
Strengths	- The ability to interpret spatial and visual information - Creative thinking – developing alternative problem-solving strategies - Tend to focus on 'big-picture' ideas, which can make them adept at understanding overarching concepts rather than getting bogged down in details - Emotional intelligence – social and people skills
Challenges	- Difficulty understanding written and numerical tasks - Organisation and planning skills - Tiredness

Chapter 11

Tourette's Syndrome

The gifts of Tourette's include an exceptional capacity for resilience, creativity, emotional depth and deep authenticity. In the long term these gifts set people up for success in careers like landscape gardening, business, sales and marketing, technology and computing, health care, research science, statistical analysis and creative arts.

These kids are often seen as twitchy and flicky, erupting with sudden movements, and are almost always incredibly self-conscious. Their sudden involuntary motor and vocal tics range from simple eye blinks, shrugs of their shoulders or grimaces to much more complex sequences that can involve bending or twisting, making sounds, or vulgar gestures or words.

Most people with Tourette's get a feeling or urge before the tic that builds up and is relieved by the movement or expression of sound. A rough parallel for someone without Tourette's might be feeling you are about to sneeze and trying to stifle it. You may know how distracting a sneeze can be, how much effort can go into suppressing one, and how most efforts result in failure. These urges are linked to activity in brain regions involved in sensory processing and motor control, such as the insula and somatosensory cortex.

Most parents notice tics by the time their child reaches about six years of age.

Discovering the neuroadvantages of Tourette's

The brain patterns of children with Tourette's commonly include variations in the functioning of:

- the basal ganglia, particularly the caudate nucleus and putamen, which play a central role in motor control and habit formation
- the thalamus, which acts as a relay station for sensory and motor signals, and often shows structural abnormalities in individuals with Tourette's syndrome
- the corpus callosum, which connects the left and right hemispheres of the brain, and may show structural abnormalities.

Tourette's can co-occur with obsessive compulsive disorder (OCD), which may also be expressed as perfectionism.

How parents can help

The social embarrassment that plagues many kids with Tourette's can be a dominating force in their lives. As much as possible, we want to help kids normalise their tics and also value themselves as smart and successful people.

Some of the actions associated with Tourette's are amplified by stress, so the ongoing development of calming techniques is helpful. Hypnosis is often extremely useful.

Many kids with Tourette's syndrome have co-occurring conditions such as obsessive compulsive disorder (OCD), attention issues or ADHD, anxiety and depression. Developing their executive functions, which include skills like planning, decision-making and impulse control, helps to set them up for long-term success. Strategies to do this are outlined in Part 2 of this book.

It is important for parents and teachers to de-stigmatise Tourette's for other children in school and in social settings. Alerting people helps to lessen sudden, negative reactions.

As you will see later in this chapter, several new gizmos, technology and methods exist that help these kids to overcome challenges and to be successful.

Step 1: Find their learning strengths

Go to www.mylearningstrengths.com and complete the analysis of learning strengths.

Neuroadvantages of kids with Tourette's

Thinking and logic
- ✓ Good problem-solving skills
- ✓ Adaptable and creative thinking
- ✓ Logical thinking

Planning and sequencing
- ✓ Advocacy for change and justice

Concentration and memory
- ✓ Usually very good memory for specific events and details

Perceptual-motor skills
- ✓ Need to move and relax
- ✓ Awareness can increase skills levels
- ✓ High skills in sports and dance that involve rapid shifts of movement

Tourette's

People smarts
- ✓ Emotional intelligence
- ✓ Social sensitivity

Language and word smarts
- ✓ Verbal communication
- ✓ Storytelling
- ✓ Debating

Spatial reasoning
- ✓ Pattern-recognition skills
- ✓ Can be applied to visual problems
- ✓ Imagination

Number smarts
- ✓ Strong pattern recognition
- ✓ Coding
- ✓ Mathematical formulas

© Andrew Fuller, *Neuroadvantage: The Strengths-based Approach to Neurodivergence* (Amba Press, 2025)

Step 2: Build on their learning strengths

We create success for our children when we start from what is strong.

Use your child's top two learning strengths and combine this knowledge with the information below to start building their neuroadvantage.

Spatial reasoning

The combination of sensory awareness and motor control challenges often gives these kids the ability to think in pictures and shapes and the interrelationship between objects. This gives them an advantage in design, puzzles, drawing and hand-eye coordination.

This can be developed further through model-building, art and design, robotics and coding.

Games like building with blocks, mazes, tangrams, Minecraft, Tetris and Monument Valley develop this.

Using visual and hands-on aids will help these kids grasp mathematical concepts.

Kids with Tourette's often bring enthusiasm and vitality to their activities, making them dynamic and motivated contributors in various fields.

While it might seem daunting, finding a physical activity that they enjoy, such as dance, sports or hands-on science experiments can help them.

Perceptual-motor skills

Perceptual-motor skills are a critical learning strength for these kids. Their bodies are urging them to act frequently. They can develop strong motor skills in specific contexts where they can channel their movements in a controlled and rhythmic manner. These need to be in areas they are interested in, such as music, dance, martial arts, yoga and sport.

Activities like archery or bowling also allow them to practise and streamline repetitive movements. Drumming, balance boards, obstacle courses and rhythm-based movement games can build this learning strength further. Others will excel in tai chi, yoga and martial arts.

To achieve this, they need discreet movement breaks and many repetitions to privately practise. Frequent breaks allow them to release energy and manage tics.

In school they often benefit from alternative seating arrangements (such as movable or wobble seats) to reduce stress and tiredness from suppressing tics. Providing pencil grips or using adaptive keyboards and speech-to-text can overcome barriers. Pool noodles beneath their feet can allow their feet to move and calm.

At home, virtual reality or motion-based video games such as Wii Sports and VR painting apps are great for the whole family. Weighted blankets, quiet spaces and using favourite tactile materials also help.

Concentration and memory

The amount of effort that these kids put into containing their tics is heroic. However, it comes at the cost of their concentration. As it is hard to remember information they can't focus on, this impacts on their learning.

For this reason alone, we want to develop this learning strength for these kids. There will be times when they need to take a break from containing their tics. Relaxation breaks are powerful. It is important to know that relaxation for many of them is not sitting still but being active, releasing energy and not suppressing tics.

Some kids find an impending tic to be so distracting that they lose focus. In this case we might ask the child to tic briefly before delivering essential information.

We can build this learning strength further by managing the amount of incoming stimulation. Noise-cancelling headphones or earbuds are incredibly helpful.

Fidget spinners and stress balls allow them to release energy without disrupting others.

Planning and sequencing

It is important to extend this learning strength for these kids. They are used to having plans and sequences interrupted by tics. We can extend this by ensuring that they return to tasks and activities after a tic. It is also helpful to create long-term plans for developing skills and abilities.

Planning tic management is a process that will take time and refinement. Observe patterns, times and conditions when tics are most likely and have a plan for dealing with them.

Thinking and logic

The adaptability required to manage tics is parallelled by an ability to think quickly, adaptively and creatively. Kids with this learning strength often demonstrate innovative problem-solving skills. Their creativity can be expressed in artistic, literary or musical forms.

Encourage creative expression and try to embark on projects that capture their interest and imagination, using these as a basis for deepening their thoughtfulness around issues.

People smarts

These kids are attuned to themselves and others in a way that very few people are. Their sensitivity to an oncoming tic gives them a level of insight into how they are feeling and also how quickly feelings can change in other people.

They are often good 'people readers' who can become great friends and intriguing conversationalists. When they develop this learning strength further, they show strong leadership and advocacy skills, often becoming advocates for themselves and others with similar conditions.

Sadly, kids with Tourette's stand out and can become the target of bullies. Developing skills to deflect bullies' mean comments and to build strong supportive friendships is protective. Developing an 'elevator pitch' to briefly explain Tourette's to others can reduce stigma.

Two examples are:

> *'My brain sometimes sends extra signals that make my body move or make sounds without me choosing to. It's called Tourette's, and I can't always control it, but it's not dangerous or on purpose. It's just how my brain works!'*

> *'My brain is like a hiccup machine, but instead of hiccups, it sometimes makes me move or make sounds without asking me first! I can't always stop it, but it's just part of how my brain works.'*

Language and word smarts

Verbal fluency and a rich vocabulary are quite common in kids with tics. Combine this with their adaptable creativity and we have kids who can engage in creative storytelling, convey rich emotionally attuned poetry, and become songwriters.

Many also display quick thinking and complex problem-solving skills. The presence of tics can interfere with writing, especially under timed conditions. We need to adapt the environment to help these kids be as successful as possible. Providing additional time in school assessments is often needed to assess what these kids are truly capable of.

This learning strength can be developed further by exposing these kids to as many forms of literature as possible. An aim can be to help them become a truly literate person – someone who can 'read deeply, think deeply, and feel deeply', as was stated by Professor Maryanne Wolf, the author of *Reader, Come Home: The Reading Brain in a Digital World* (2018).

Number smarts

While tics can interfere with learning, many kids with Tourette's have strengths in spatial reasoning and pattern recognition that underpin parts of mathematics. Their capacity for innovative problem-solving and numerical reasoning can be strengthened by using graphs, diagrams and physical objects like blocks and dice to represent abstract concepts.

Using maths games and apps such as Prodigy and Mathletics can help build sustained engagement.

Leveraging their strengths with gizmos, tech and methods

Learning

- **Dragon NaturallySpeaking.** This speech-to-text software allows kids to dictate their thoughts and have them converted into written text. This is particularly useful for kids whose tics interfere with writing.
- **Google Voice Typing.** A free, built-in speech-to-text tool available in Google Docs, this allows students to dictate their writing, helping them bypass challenges with handwriting or typing.
- **Khan Academy.** This program provides a structured series of mathematics lessons.
- **NaturalReader.** A text-to-speech app that reads aloud text from documents, web pages or PDFs, this can help kids with Tourette's who have difficulty with reading due to tics or associated attention issues. It converts text into spoken words with natural-sounding voices, and is available in multiple languages.

Calming

- **Breathe2Relax.** This is a stress-management app that focuses on diaphragmatic breathing exercises to reduce stress and anxiety. These breathing exercises can help calm the nervous system and potentially reduce the intensity of tics.
- **Calm.** This is a mindfulness app that offers meditation, breathing exercises, and sleep stories to help manage anxiety and stress. It provides tools for relaxation, sleep improvement and managing anxiety, which can indirectly help reduce tic severity.
- **Headspace.** This is a mindfulness and meditation app that can help reduce stress and anxiety, which are often associated with Tourette's and can exacerbate tics. It offers guided meditations, breathing exercises and relaxation techniques designed to help users manage stress and maintain mental well-being.

Organisation and planning

- **Focus@Will.** A music app designed to improve focus and productivity by playing music that is scientifically optimised to help with concentration, this can be helpful for kids with Tourette's and ADHD. It includes customisable channels of music that are designed to enhance focus and reduce distractions.
- **Habitica.** This is a habit-building and productivity app that gamifies tasks and habits. While not specifically for tics, it can help kids track and manage premonitory urges by turning management strategies into daily habits. Users can create tasks, set goals and earn rewards for completing them, which can encourage the use of techniques learned in therapy to manage tics.

Virtual reality (VR) and augmented reality (AR)

- **FitMi Home Therapy.** A home therapy tool designed to improve strength, coordination and fine motor skills, this can be beneficial for students with motor tics. Customised exercises that target different areas of the body help improve overall motor function.
- **Forest.** This is a productivity app that helps users stay focused on tasks by growing virtual trees. If the user leaves the app before the set focus time is up, the tree dies. Focus and time management are encouraged through visual rewards.

- **Tourette Association of America App.** This provides resources, support and a community for individuals with Tourette's and their families.

Parenting priorities for kids with Tourette's

Big impacts
- accepting that your child is smart and that their tics have nothing to do with their capacity to succeed
- believing in them and working with them to develop plans.

Quick fixes
- learning calming techniques.

Waste of time
- trying to suppress tics or control them.

If it's not one thing, it could also be another

Many of these issues have intersections and overlaps. Movement coordination is commonly seen in kids with Tourette's, kids on the spectrums and kids with dyspraxia. It is interesting to speculate if the motor areas of the brain may share some variations that account for this – in particular, the movement pathways of the motor cortex, the basal ganglia and the cerebellum, as well as the pathways regulating dopamine in the brain.

Similarities between Tourette's and the spectrums	
Strengths	• Strong spatial reasoning and analytical skills, useful in fields like mathematics, engineering and design • Creative and original thinking • Generating innovative ideas in storytelling, music or art • Empathy and authenticity, especially when connecting with people who share their interests

Challenges	• Difficulties with social communication (from the spectrums) combined with the visibility of tics (from Tourette's) can lead to peer rejection or bullying • Managing frustration, anxiety or anger • Negative perceptions of tics and social misunderstandings can lead to low self-esteem and a reluctance to participate in social or academic activities • Conditions like anxiety, depression and obsessive-compulsive behaviours are common in both the spectrums and Tourette's, amplifying challenges

About 60 per cent of kids with Tourette's also have attention issues or ADHD.

Similarities between Tourette's and attention issues	
Strengths	• Good verbal skills • Quick creative thinking • Energy and enthusiasm
Challenges	• Timing and sequencing of motor tasks • Working memory, making it harder to hold and manipulate numbers or steps in mind • Disruptions in sustaining concentration and sequential problem-solving • Overwhelmed by too much stimulation • Provide access to sensory tools
Similarities between Tourette's and sensory sensitivities	
Strengths	• Have creative problem-solving abilities and think outside the box • Heightened awareness of details in art, music or storytelling, enhancing their creative expression • A knack for storytelling, debates or persuasive speech
Challenges	• Hypersensitivity to stimuli (e.g., noise, light, textures), leading to distraction, distress or meltdowns • Combined with Tourette's tics, sensory challenges may amplify physical and emotional fatigue, impacting focus and academic performance • Motor and vocal tics can disrupt concentration, social interactions and physical tasks • Challenges in organisation, planning and self-regulation • Avoidance behaviours may develop in response to fear of sensory discomfort or social judgment

Similarities between Tourette's and defiance	
Strengths	- Problem-solving skills and resilience - Determination, particularly when pursuing their interests or goals - Honesty, loyalty and friendship
Challenges	- Difficulty regulating emotions, leading to frequent outbursts or intense reactions - Tics and defiant behaviour can create social misunderstandings, leading to peer rejection or strained relationships - Tics and frequent conflict with authority can lead to anxiety and feelings of inadequacy, especially if they face stigma or criticism

Similarities between Tourette's and movement issues	
Strengths	- Creative thinking and finding innovative solutions to problems - Verbal communication and language skills - Attention to detail when physical coordination is not required, such as analysing text or brainstorming ideas
Challenges	- Dyspraxia affects motor coordination, making tasks like handwriting or participating in physical education difficult. Motor tics from Tourette's add to these challenges, leading to frustration and fatigue - Executive functioning issues with planning, organisation and working memory - Struggles with spatial awareness - Dyspraxia-related difficulties in spatial reasoning can affect activities like drawing, map reading, and understanding visual-spatial concepts – these challenges can extend to maths and science tasks requiring spatial visualisation

Similarities between Tourette's and dysgraphia	
Strengths	- Enhanced creativity, excelling in storytelling, problem-solving and artistic endeavours - Strong verbal skills – oral storytelling, debates or presentations - Empathy and connection with others
Challenges	- Handwriting and written expression - Executive functioning challenges in organisation, planning and time management - Anxiety and perfectionism

Similarities between Tourette's and dyscalculia	
Strengths	- Enhanced creativity and problem-solving - Strong verbal skills – verbal reasoning and oral communication - Pattern recognition in non-numerical contexts – excel in identifying patterns in language, music or visuals
Challenges	- Understanding mathematics – dyscalculia impairs the ability to understand number relationships, sequencing and spatial reasoning, making maths tasks particularly challenging - Tics can disrupt concentration, making it harder to focus on complex problem-solving tasks - Executive function challenges in concentration, working memory and planning - Difficulty organising multi-step processes can hinder performance in tasks requiring logical progression - Tiredness and frustration – the combined effort required to manage tics and compensate for maths difficulties can cause mental fatigue and decreased motivation

Chapter 12
Auditory Processing Issues

One of the main gifts of auditory processing issues is the ability to observe astutely, think deeply and interpret the world in creative ways.

These kids hear normally, but sounds become jumbled inside their brains. There was an old song that said, 'Everybody's talking at me, I don't hear a word they're saying'. This is the world of these kids.

Misunderstandings result from how the brain interprets and processes sounds. They often have difficulty listening in noisy areas, keeping track of people who talk fast or indistinctly, and following complex verbal instructions. Even when they try really, really hard to understand what is being said to them, they get mixed up and find it hard to follow instructions.

Words that are quite similar – such as cat, sat, bat and mat – most easily get mixed up.

It is hard to be socially successful if you can't really understand what is being said by friends. When it is hard to comprehend what is going on, it is easy to become frustrated, bored, angry, sad or ashamed. Understandably, some of these kids feel embarrassed and cover up by distracting others or becoming the class clown in school.

This can look to other people a lot like poor concentration, low motivation and poor organisational skills, but really they just haven't understood what is being said to them.

Schools are full of words. As a result, these kids become saturated with verbal overload. At times it can feel impossible to help them to be successful, but with some creative thinking, it can be done. When you mix up sounds in your head, it can be a lot of work to read and to write. This makes school, and trying to keep track of what people are saying, incredibly tiring. It is also hard to remember information that doesn't make sense to you. To some teachers these kids can appear daydreamy, inattentive and unmotivated.

Between 5 and 10 per cent of students have these issues. Another 16 per cent of students in schools have hearing limitations due to ear infections, colds or flus. These issues affect the learning of up to one in four students.

While there are challenges, the gift of auditory processing issues can set these kids up for success. It is a bit like unlocking a door.

Discovering the neuroadvantages of auditory processing issues

The brain patterns of children with auditory processing issues commonly include variations in the functioning of:

- the primary auditory cortex, located in the temporal lobe, which is responsible for processing sound information
- the corpus callosum, the structure that connects the left and right hemispheres of the brain, which plays a crucial role in the integration of auditory information
- the planum temporale, which is an area of the brain associated with auditory processing and language.

Research has shown that individuals with auditory processing issues often perform poorly in dichotic listening tasks, where different sounds are presented to each ear simultaneously, indicating difficulties in processing and integrating auditory information from both ears. This deficit is particularly pronounced when processing speech sounds.

How parents can help

Begin with an audiologist's assessment to ensure your child's hearing is ok. They will be able to give you information about the specific types of sounds your child struggles to make sense of. We need to differentiate what is being heard clearly from what can be understood.

This is an area of neurodivergence where a clear diagnosis is especially helpful. Otherwise, these kids incorrectly label themselves as slow and stupid. Other adults can incorrectly conclude they are lazy or inattentive.

Neuroadvantages of kids with auditory processing issues

Planning and sequencing
- ✓ Visual planning and sequencing

Thinking and logic
- ✓ Creative problem-solving
- ✓ Imaginative solutions

Concentration and memory
- ✓ Proficient with visual information, not as successful with verbal information

People smarts
- ✓ Loyal friends who are sensitive to others

Perceptual-motor skills
- ✓ Skilled at dance, sport and construction

Language and word smarts
- ✓ Creative communication
- ✓ Emotionally rich writing

Spatial reasoning
- ✓ Construction
- ✓ Design
- ✓ Art
- ✓ Layout

Number smarts
- ✓ Hands-on, practical mathematical problem-solving

© Andrew Fuller, *Neuroadvantage: The Strengths-based Approach to Neurodivergence* (Amba Press, 2025)

As much as you can, lessen the amount of background noise at home. Having sound on in the background will make it difficult to communicate with your child.

If you are unable to dampen the sounds in your house, take your child to the quietest part of the house to deliver important information. Avoid tiled areas that can bounce sound around.

Move fairly close to your child, make eye contact, and ensure they can see your lips move as you say words. Stand so your face is well lit. Make short statements. Check what has been heard by asking them to summarise what you have said.

If they have misheard or misunderstood you, repeat your statement once using precisely the same words. Sometimes, in an attempt to understand, children gloss over some words, so repeating gives them a chance to fill in the words they didn't understand.

If they are still misunderstanding your messages, restate the message using different words.

Be patient. You are building listening and understanding skills. This will take time.

In the rush hours of family life (getting up in the morning and getting into bed on time) stick to routines where over time kids get to learn the sequence of what needs to be done. Aim to have routines with as few verbal instructions as possible. For example, an instruction like 'Jack, time to get ready for bed' should ideally set into action a routine that involves teeth-brushing and pyjama-wearing.

It takes at least six weeks to develop a routine. For each step of the routine, you'll need to prompt your child. For example:

Jack, time to get ready for bed.

First we need to brush teeth.

Then we need to put on pyjamas.

Next we need to get into bed.

Now after a story I'll switch the light off.

It's now time for sleep.

Boost hearing and understanding with games and stories. Games like 'Simon says' and musical chairs teach listening strategies and provide a chance to practise. Audiobooks, choose-your-own-adventure stories, and Reader's Theatre, where particular words are matched with specific movements, also help.

In terms of school, the more that you can help your child's teacher understand the nature of your child's auditory issues, the better. It is very easy for some teachers to mis-assess your child's behaviour as rudeness or lack of interest.

Schools with open learning areas are always a disaster for these kids. Teachers need to summarise the main points frequently and to set shorter assignments or allow for more time.

As you will see later, several new gizmos and methods exist that help these kids to overcome challenges and to be successful.

Step 1: Find their learning strengths

Go to www.mylearningstrengths.com and complete the analysis of learning strengths.

Step 2: Build on their learning strengths

Spatial reasoning

Kids with auditory issues often have learning strengths related to thinking in pictures. Others have particular skills in construction or in artistic or mechanical design. While their problem-solving skills may not be expressed in words, they can assemble objects in the right order to build things. While the analysis of their learning strengths is a helpful starting point, it is then a matter of watching what they can do rather than waiting for them to tell you what they can do.

We can extend this learning strength by giving them puzzles to solve, model assembly, building and mechanical constructions.

Perceptual-motor skills

A young man who attended our clinic could barely conduct a coherent conversation but could point out accurately the most minuscule insect climbing up the branch of a tree. These kids can have exquisitely sensitive awareness of the non-verbal world.

Many of them also develop great skills in sports and dance. Coaching them involves fewer words and more demonstrations. Showing slow-motion video clips of people performing a skill they wish to improve on is highly effective.

This learning strength can be expanded by involving them in painting, sculpting, dance and graphic design.

Some also develop strong non-verbal communication skills, including the ability to interpret body language, facial expressions and visual cues.

Concentration and memory

There are three main ways information becomes stored in our memory: through what we see, what we hear and how we move (also known as muscle memory). Of these, what we see – our visual pathway – is the most powerful. Kids with auditory processing issues often develop strong abilities in visually focusing.

We can develop learning strengths in this area by picking out the most important information when presented visually, and processing information into mind maps, concept maps or physical sequences of movements. Using cartoons and pictures, having young people take photos of objects or ideas that they want to remember, and visual note-taking all build this area.

Planning and sequencing

The ability of these kids to organise a series of verbal instructions or ideas into a coherent plan is often quite poor. Using visual objects such as Post-it notes and arranging them in a logical order overcomes this. Mapping tools like Kidspiration and Inspiration can also help with this.

We can extend this area by involving them in planning constructions or STEM/STEAM subjects in school.

People smarts

While the meaning of some words will elude many of them, they can be sensitively attuned 'people readers'. Their own struggles in deciphering what is going on makes most of them kind and considerate people.

As they can misinterpret what people say, developing people-reading skills including body language and micro-expressions will be incredibly beneficial in their lives. For some, not being distracted by words can mean they become incredibly astute and emotionally intelligent.

Language and word smarts

Kids with auditory processing issues often develop the ability to create vivid stories with emotional richness.

They are also attentive to information they see, which makes them good at editing, and interpreting or creating nuances in literature. As a result, they are often adept at analysing the metaphors and symbolism in texts.

Number smarts

When mathematical concepts are shown to them using hands-on experiential learning (blocks, dice, puzzles, pizza slices and so on), these kids are skilled at thinking numerically. Their preference for learning through either seeing or doing rather than hearing results in strong pattern recognition in areas like geometry, modelling, design and mechanical reasoning.

Often they thrive in this area when steps are shown to them in a clear sequential order.

They tend to prefer formulas, procedures and step-by-step processes.

Leveraging their strengths with gizmos, tech and methods

Learning

- **Blending Board.** This is a phonics app that helps kids with auditory issues practise blending sounds into words, which is essential for developing reading and spelling skills. It includes customisable blending exercises that focus on improving phonemic awareness and decoding skills.
- **Dragon NaturallySpeaking.** This is a speech-recognition program that converts spoken words into text, allowing kids with auditory issues to take notes or write papers without relying on listening to and processing speech. It offers high-accuracy speech-to-text conversion with the ability to control the computer using voice commands.

- **Earobics.** This is an interactive program designed to improve auditory processing skills through games and exercises that target phonological awareness, auditory discrimination and auditory sequencing. It includes activities that adapt to the kid's skill level, focusing on developing the auditory skills necessary for reading and listening comprehension.
- **Fast ForWord.** A comprehensive language and reading intervention program, this focuses on strengthening the cognitive skills necessary for reading and listening, including auditory processing, attention and memory. It offers exercises that adapt to the kid's performance, focusing on areas like phonemic awareness, sound discrimination and listening comprehension.
- **HearBuilder Auditory Memory.** This is an educational program that focuses on improving auditory memory, which is crucial for following directions and retaining verbal information. It includes interactive games that teach kids how to remember and recall numbers, words, sentences and stories.
- **Immersive Reader.** This tool reads text aloud to users and allows them to control how it is presented. It's available in Microsoft Edge, PowerPoint, Word and OneNote.
- **LACE (Listening and Communication Enhancement): Purpose.** This program is designed to improve listening and communication skills, particularly in challenging auditory environments like noisy classrooms. It includes exercises that train the brain to improve speech.
- **Lindamood-Bell Auditory Processing Programs.** These focus on phonemic awareness and auditory discrimination.
- **Lindamood Phoneme Sequencing Program (LiPS).** This focuses on developing phonemic awareness by teaching kids to recognise and manipulate the sounds within words. Research supports its effectiveness in improving auditory discrimination, decoding and reading comprehension.
- **Orton-Gillingham Approach.** This is a multisensory method for teaching reading and phonics, incorporating auditory, visual and kinaesthetic learning. It is particularly effective for children with auditory issues who also have dyslexia or other language-based learning disabilities.

- **Phoneme Factory Sound Sorter.** This app is designed to help kids with auditory issues improve their auditory discrimination and phonological awareness by sorting and identifying different phonemes. It includes games and activities that focus on sound discrimination, which is critical for understanding speech and improving reading skills.
- **'Simon says' game apps.** These are digital versions of the classic 'Simon says' game. They require kids to listen carefully and follow auditory instructions, helping improve auditory attention and sequencing.
- **Sound matching games (e.g., Tots Play).** These matching games focus on identifying and matching sounds, helping to improve auditory discrimination and memory in a playful manner.
- **Speech-to-text tools.** These allow the child to focus on content rather than struggling to process spoken information.
- **The Listening Program (TLP).** This uses music-based training to improve auditory processing and focus.

Calming

- **Brainwaves: 35 Binaural Series.** This comprises advanced binaural brainwave 'entrainment' programs for focus, relaxation, sleep, anxiety and meditation.
- **Headspace for Kids.** This is a mindfulness app offering guided meditation and relaxation exercises tailored for children, helping them manage anxiety and focus better. It offers short, kid-friendly meditation sessions that teach techniques for calming the mind and improving focus.
- **Smiling Mind.** A mindfulness app that offers guided meditation programs for different age groups, this helps students with auditory issues to reduce stress and improve concentration.
- **The Mindfulness App.** This helps users enjoy a more restful sleep, stress less, and reduce their anxiety.

Organisation and planning

- **AudioNote.** A note-taking app that synchronises audio recordings with written notes, this helps kids with auditory issues review and reinforce what was said during class. It has the ability to record

lectures while taking notes, with the recording linked to the notes for easy playback and review.
- **Notability.** This is a note-taking app that allows kids to record audio while taking notes, with the option to play back the recording and match it with their notes, clarifying points they may have missed.

Communication

- **Bone conduction headphones.** These transmit sound directly to the cochlea, bypassing the outer and middle ear, for clearer auditory input. They are beneficial for children with specific auditory sensitivities or deficits.
- **Integrated Listening Systems (iLs).** These tools combine sound therapy with movement to improve auditory and sensory integration.
- **Personal FM systems (e.g., Phonak Roger Pen and Roger Focus).** These are wireless devices that transmit the teacher's voice directly to the student's ear. They reduce background noise and enhance speech clarity, making it easier for students to focus on the speaker's voice. They are widely supported by research for improving speech perception and reducing listening effort among children with APD.
- **Pocketalker Ultra.** This is a personal amplifier that helps kids with auditory issues hear more clearly in one-on-one conversations or small group settings. It is a portable, easy-to-use device with adjustable volume and tone controls, helping to amplify the speaker's voice and reduce background noise.
- **SoundAMP R.** An app that amplifies sound and enhances speech clarity, this turns an iPhone or iPad into a personal amplifier.
- **Sound field amplification systems.** These are classroom-based systems where the teacher's voice is amplified and transmitted directly, minimising background noise. Studies show that sound field systems improve listening comprehension, attention and academic performance, especially in noisy classrooms. They include adjustable amplification levels and the ability to filter out background noise, helping kids with auditory issues hear speech more clearly in various environments.
- **Synthesia.** This AI-driven video-creation tool produces high-quality, engaging videos from text.
- **Voiceitt.** This provides AI-based speech recognition for non-standard speech.

Parenting priorities for kids with auditory processing issues

Big impacts
- visual aids, hands-on activities and auditory tools like text-to-speech software
- leveraging their interests
- using assistive technology.

Quick fixes
- breaking tasks into smaller, manageable steps
- using visual schedules, diagrams, flowcharts and mind maps to aid comprehension.

Waste of time
- lots of words
- background noise
- distractions
- complex verbal instructions.

If it's not one thing, it could also be another

Similarities between auditory processing issues and the spectrums	
Strengths	- Spatial and visual reasoning - Good memory - Creative problem-solving
Challenges	- Difficulty processing and understanding spoken language - Social communication - Executive functions – planning, organising, switching between tasks, generalising ideas to other settings
Similarities between auditory processing and attention issues	
Strengths	- Enthusiasm and energy - Visual learning - Strong focus on areas of interest

Challenges	• Difficulty following and understanding verbal instructions • Sustaining concentration • Becoming overwhelmed in noisy environments
Similarities between auditory processing and sensory processing issues	
Strengths	• Visual learning and creativity • Attention and sensitivity to details • Spatial reasoning
Challenges	• Sensory overload • Challenges with concentration and focus • Executive functions – planning, concentration and memory, organisation
Similarities between auditory processing issues and defiance	
Strengths	• Acute observational skills • Sense of justice and fairness • Potential for leadership
Challenges	• Slower processing of information (especially verbal) • Social relationships • Executive functions – impulse control, emotional regulation
Similarities between auditory processing and movement issues	
Strengths	• Non-verbal learning and spatial reasoning • Creative problem-solving • Adaptability
Challenges	• Following verbal instructions and sequences • Executive functions – memory, emotional regulation • Low self-esteem
Similarities between auditory processing issues and dysgraphia	
Strengths	• Strength of oral presentations and storytelling • Spatial reasoning • Creativity
Challenges	• Difficulty putting thoughts into written words • Executive functions – memory, emotional regulation • Anxiety

Similarities between auditory processing issues and dyscalculia	
Strengths	- Strengths in narrative thinking - Attention to detail - Spatial reasoning - Creative thinking
Challenges	- Maths anxiety and numerical reasoning - Following the steps and sequences in problem-solving - Frustration and avoidance - Anxiety - Noisy distracting settings
Similarities between auditory processing issues and Tourette's	
Strengths	- Strong nonverbal communication skills - People smarts - Perceptual-motor and spatial learning strengths – frequently excel in visual or hands-on learning environments
Challenges	- Auditory processing difficulties make it challenging to process spoken instructions and to follow conversations; combined with Tourette's, this can lead to frequent misunderstandings and difficulty keeping up with verbal information - Concentration and attention challenges – background noise or rapid speech may exacerbate these challenges, leading to frustration - Academic performance – verbal-heavy tasks, such as lectures, oral instructions or discussions, can be particularly challenging - Difficulties with auditory memory and comprehension can impact subjects like reading comprehension, maths word problems, or foreign language learning

Tan, L. (1999). *Auditory Processing at School*, Listening Works.

Part 2
Executive Functions

Chapter 13

Setting Up Your Neurodivergent Child for Success in Life

Having discussed in this book how to convert neurodivergence into neuroadvantage, I now want to discuss the longer-term process of helping your child grow towards success.

The big six skills of success

There are six skills that predict success for neurodivergent children and teens. Parents, teachers and young people themselves can all play a role in building these skills. The big six skills put us in the 'driver's seat' of life, rather than being a passenger directed by others, and are collectively known as 'executive functions'.

These skills are:

1. **Planning** – constructing plans and implementing them
2. **Concentration** – directing attention and focusing on the important aspects of an issue
3. **Memory** – remembering information such as the steps in solving a mathematical problem
4. **Impulse control** – this is the 'pause' button of life and allows us to think before we act
5. **Cognitive flexibility** – being able to change your thinking when needed
6. **Emotional regulation** – settling yourself when upset and calming yourself when stressed.

Having these skills turns out to be pretty handy – it predicts achievement, health, wealth and quality of life more powerfully than either IQ or socio-economic status.

Having at least some of these skills enables your child to be ready for school and to succeed once they get there.

The importance of these skills does not end in childhood. They are crucial for success in getting and keeping jobs, making and keeping friends, establishing good relationships, weight control, staying out of jail and resisting drug abuse. Adults with these skills are happier and have a better quality of life.

Building the six skills

We all start out in life being fairly impulse-driven and easily upset, with flighty concentration and limited memory. As we mature and as our frontal lobes kick into gear, we generally improve in most of these areas. When parents and teachers work to develop them, the gains are substantial.

It's not all smooth sailing though. Impulse control is not always at its best in the early teen years. Planning can go missing at times. Our organisational skills don't peak until our mid-twenties. We've all had days when our ability to calm and settle ourselves has been a bit patchy.

While generally we all get better at these skills as we mature, if you put a bit of stress into the mix and add some tiredness and a fear of getting something wrong, our functioning dips fairly dramatically.

These are the skills that give neurodivergent kids the opportunity to create success and independence on their terms. As neurodivergent kids are sometimes quirky and always individuals, we need to tailor our approach to each child.

Our aim is to help your child develop the skills to be as independent as possible. To achieve this, we need to take our time to discover the intersection between different aspects of their lives:

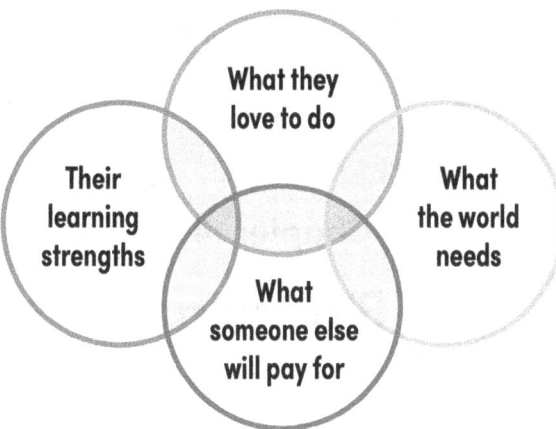

Locating the intersection of these points guides people towards finding the mission and purpose in their lives.

Chapter 14

Planning

The future belongs to those who plan for it.

Being able to plan and sequence steps towards a desired outcome powerfully predicts success in life.

With this ability, you can organise what you need to do, get things done in the right order, make decisions and plans, and carry them out. When you apply your determination, you will stick with things that are hard until they are done.

Being able to plan in a world that is reactive and impulsive is like possessing a secret power.

It is helpful to talk to kids along the lines of 'If we want to do … what are we going to need to do to get there? What do we do first? … second, etc.'

Helping your child develop planning skills

The big method is called 'Imagine forwards, plan backwards'.

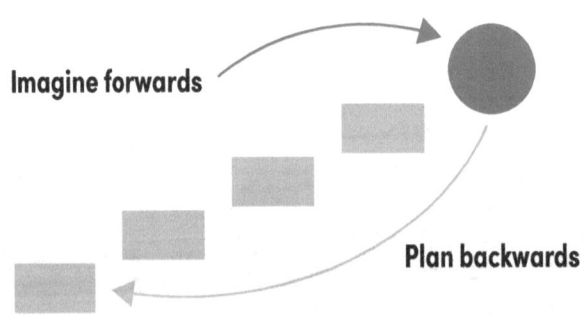

In this process you help your child identify an outcome they would like. Outline it as clearly as possible. Then, working backwards, work out the steps towards achieving that outcome.

What would be happening if you weren't quite there but almost?
What would have happened just before that?
Go right back to wherever your starting point is.

Activities that build planning skills
- basic music and language training
- creating a picture in your head of the goal(s) you are after
- fashion design and jewellery-making
- art, pottery, sculpture
- juggling
- dancing.

Family strategies that build planning skills
- involving children in planning events, outings, holidays, shopping trips
- using sticky notes and ordering them into the steps of a process
- using visual planners
- creating a wall calendar
- developing checklists for common activities
- cooking.

Games that build planning skills
- mazes
- Meccano
- checkers
- chess
- dominos
- Lego
- building towers with cards or pipe cleaners
- kite construction and flying
- origami
- designing and building a skate ramp
- strategy games: chess, Monopoly, Risk
- backgammon
- card games
- marbles.

Chapter 15

Concentration

Our concentration is hard to gain and easy to lose. Learning how to gain it, keep it and shift it appropriately is a major advantage in learning and in life.

At times we want our concentration to have pinpoint accuracy. At other times we need a broader awareness. A simple example is crossing the road: we need to be focused on the cars approaching us, and we also need to be alert for cars pulling over unexpectedly. In classrooms there are some times when we need to take a broader perspective and other times when we need to focus on our own work.

It is hard to succeed in life if our mind flits about and wanders. It is hard to learn something new if our mind remains focused elsewhere.

Anyone who has ever learned to drive a car, play a musical instrument or juggle multiple demands in a day knows that we often improve after some practice. Concentration is a skill we can all improve at.

While some kids are vague and completely unfocused, most kids are simply focused on areas that we might consider irrelevant. This may either be because they can't yet filter out distractions, or more often, because they are focused on something else. One of the rules of thumb of concentration is: what attracts our attention can also distract us. This is why building from learning strengths works.

With these kids, if you don't have eye contact, you don't have their attention. Use physical signals and movements to indicate that it is now time to focus and to emphasise key ideas.

Helping your child develop concentration skills

The goal is for your child to be asking, 'What is the most important thing to concentrate on at this moment?' and 'What is the most important part of this to remember?'

Hobbies and collections build concentration. Some neurodivergent kids are great collectors of things: bottle tops, stamps, dolls, war-gaming figures, football cards, Lego pieces, cuddly toys, golf balls, marbles, and sometimes, worms. You find weird things they have picked up in their pockets. Their bedrooms often contain a growing exhibition of objects.

Activities that build concentration
- photos that remind them of past successes
- glitter pens, paints and crayons to make note-taking exciting
- gymnastics
- Lego, building models, Meccano sets, constructing and painting small figures
- learning knitting or sewing
- sports
- Rubik's cubes, mazes
- constructing and flying kites
- playing battleships, checkers, chess.

Family strategies that build concentration
- reminders such as 'Pack your lunch!'
- coloured pieces of paper for them to write on to assist memory
- cooking
- music training
- rock wall climbing, abseiling, orienteering, dancing
- building and driving go karts
- finding ways to connect life events
- calendars, diaries, posters, fridge magnets, family noticeboards and stickers (which are useful ways of connecting life events and developing awareness).

Games that build concentration
- Pictionary
- 'Simon says'

- jigsaw puzzles (which help motor skills, abstract reasoning and spatial organisation)
- 'I spy' games (which develop language and attention)
- the card game 'concentration'
- hands-on, concrete examples and diagrams in mathematics
- Computer games such as:
  - Farming Simulator (which allows players to work as a farmer who raises livestock and grows and sells crops to earn money – players can control farm machinery and breed animals)
  - Medal of Honor
  - Tetris
  - Monument Valley
  - Minecraft
  - Just Dance 2020, Dance Central, Dance Dance Revolution
  - Sim City (which teaches players how to focus and manage limited resources and the consequences of their decisions)
  - Microsoft Flight Simulator X (which allows players to learn the basics of flying and complete 80 missions from around the world)
  - Pokémon GO
  - Wii Fit and Wii Sports
  - Zumba Fitness: World Party.

Chapter 16

Memory

One of the strongest predictors of academic results is intelligence and one of the highest correlates of intelligence is memory.

Memory allows us to convert data into information, information into understanding and understanding into wisdom.

Memory is the basis of learning. You can't use information that you can't recall, and you can't recall what you haven't focused on. You might think, in a world that can search for almost anything on the internet, 'Why would I bother developing my memory?'

Developing memory as a learning strength is like having a head start in a race.

Memory is developed in comparing, sequencing, summarising, filtering out irrelevant information, reading and solving problems. To do this, we need to build multiple pathways for taking in and practising new information.

When we work with children and teens from the areas of their learning strengths, we can broaden those strengths and catapult their success in other areas.

Helping your child develop memory skills

Memory is also particularly important for learning to read. This is why the development of memory is so important to student success.

Break down the steps involved in learning any new topic or skill into ladders of understanding, with each rung representing a different step. Use different-coloured pieces of paper for different tasks.

Most kids enjoy challenging and developing their memory, from 'What do you think your first words were?' to 'Where did you have your favourite meal?'

Keep logbooks and visual diaries and create picture books. Create visual prompts.

Have a day planner or calendar on the refrigerator. This can help you keep track of appointments and activities and can also serve as a journal in which you write anything that you would like to remember. It models to children that writing down and organising information reinforces learning and increases memory.

Learn to use prior knowledge to solve problems – always ask yourself, 'What else do I know that relates to this?'

Develop memory by focusing on learning about someone else. Notice their eye colour. Use their name when you speak to them. Remember what they tell you.

Activities that build memory

- noticing how ideas can be similar or different (e.g., finding two similarities and one difference – this increases memory)
- increasing the use of body memory (counting on fingers, using physical cues to recall something)
- using your fingers to count off the five most important ideas
- practising balancing
- dancing, songs, musical training, dominoes, bridge, poker, chess, backgammon
- mentally manipulating players on a favourite sports team (e.g., if you had to replace X, who would you choose?)
- memorising a sequence of ideas
- origami
- telling a joke or a story.

Family strategies that build memory

- creating to-do lists
- writing shopping lists
- planning family events or holidays
- playing memory games to learn the alphabet, read words, get ready on time, etc. – for example: what do you think comes next?

- remembering ten objects on a tray
- repeating key ideas to build memory – 'Repeat after me'
- playing the memory game 'concentration'
- looking at a series of pictures quickly, then closing your eyes and trying to describe them
- sorting, matching and organising tasks
- playing spot-the-difference games
- replicating models of blocks or Lego pieces – see it in your mind
- creating visual schedules and timelines
- juggling
- learning movements and poems
- playing memory games involving numbers.

Games that build memory
- playing card games such as Uno, 21 and 500
- using rhymes and stories to remember key numerical information
- playing 'Simon says'
- playing charades
- taking part in acting and theatre sports.

Chapter 17

Impulse Control

Learning that your first decision is not always your best decision is usually hard won through life. A series of scalded tongues, scraped knees, sprained ankles and banged elbows through our childhood teaches us that our impulses are not always to be trusted.

There is a developmental leap forward in anyone's life when they eventually realise that their first impulse is not always the best thing to do. Impulse control requires the development of information-processing controls.

Helping your child develop impulse control

Without impulse control, kids tend to call out, interrupt and blurt out ideas rather than consider them.

Help them to step through a problem physically. Each step taken is a different aspect of an issue they are trying to solve. At times, step in at different angles representing the different possible ways of solving the problem.

Teach kids to prioritise. This helps impulse control – for example, 'Which of these is most important? What is next most important?'

You can extend this by asking kids to rate different foods from like to dislike.

Ordering, categorising, ranking – learning to group and categorise different objects by different criteria (shape, texture, colour, function, texture) helps memory and impulse control.

Ask kids for their first idea, then their second idea and help them learn the value of impulse control and thinking again.

Guide children to anticipate outcomes: 'If you do … what do you think will happen next? Great, that's your first thought – I wonder what your second thought might be?'

Explore ideas with them. Ask 'What makes you think that?' This increases reasoning, consideration and impulse control.

Activities that build impulse control

- treasure hunts
- gardening
- cooking
- archery
- rock wall climbing
- aerobic physical education
- ping pong
- tae kwon do
- yoga
- drumming circles
- sculpture and pottery
- stop signs – use non-verbal signals to create stop, think (before doing)
- cubs, guides, scouts
- mazes
- trail-making.

Family strategies that build impulse control

- 'Stop, think, do!' – this can be visually signalled to children
- when there is a problem to solve, drawing out a sequence of pictures (or shapes) to represent the different steps involved in solving it
- finger games like 'Eensy weensy spider'
- clicking your fingers or clapping when a particular word is used
- waiting for your turn
- rhymes like 'There once was a woman who swallowed a fly …'

Games that build impulse control

- 'go no go' games such as 'Simon says'
- musical chairs
- statues
- Minecraft
- Lego, building models
- snap, Uno
- 20 questions
- strategy games
- Monument Valley
- Meccano sets, sports, jigsaw puzzles
- four square or down ball
- juggling and magic tricks
- silent indoor ball games
- Rubik's cubes, mazes
- constructing and painting small figures.

Chapter 18

Cognitive Flexibility

If not doing the first thing that comes into their mind is an issue for some impulsive kids, being able to change the direction of their own thinking is quite another. Some neurodivergent kids, once they have made their mind up, dig their heels in and stick resolutely to their decision, disregarding evidence to the contrary.

While being resolute and determined may be helpful in achieving goals, these are not always helpful attributes in negotiations and in relationships.

Being able to shift your thinking or develop cognitive flexibility is useful for problem-solving, creativity, getting along with others and managing stressful life events.

Helping your child develop cognitive flexibility

Moving a neurodivergent child is one of the most powerful ways to shift thinking. It is almost as if being in a different location helps them to think differently. This is why walking alongside an upset child is almost always better than standing or sitting still.

The change of location does not have to be major. It can be to a less-crowded room in the house or a different side of a classroom. You can use a pretext if you wish such as, 'You seem upset. Let's talk. I've just got to turn off the stove first, so come with me' or 'I just need a drink of water before we talk. Would you like one?'

Obviously, you should move to somewhere that is safe and invite rather than force a child to move.

Another method is: 'What if we tried this differently?' With this method, you might say, 'You seem upset, and I don't want you to feel that way. What could we do differently?' If a different approach doesn't come to mind, you could say, 'Maybe we both need some time to think about this. How about we take some thinking time and then get back together to talk it through?'

Most kids are patterned creatures – they do the same things, in the same way, over and over again. That means some of their actions and words are almost automatic. Parents can alter the routine by changing one small aspect of it. For example, a child comes into a room looking gloomy and upset. On many an occasion you'll say something like, 'You're looking upset. What's happened?' (*what* – 'What has happened?' is always a more important word than *why* – 'Why are feeling upset?'). Every so often, you might greet a gloomy child with an upbeat, 'Guess what? I've got some great news for you!'

A third method is to play dice with your thinking. We all get locked into our thoughts and methods of problem-solving sometimes. One way to shift our thinking is to roll a dice to determine how we are going to talk about something or think about it. This builds flexibility and creativity.

Play dice with your thinking:

1	Think it is the world's biggest problem	4	Think about it like it is a future problem
2	Think about it as already solved	5	Think about it like it happened a long time ago
3	Think about what is missing	6	Think about it like there are many solutions to this problem.

Activities that build cognitive flexibility

The 'Yes, and …' game:

- Start a story: 'Today was difficult because …'
- The next person responds with 'Yes, and …', then adds to the story.
- Continue for a few turns without saying 'No, but …'

This helps train the brain to build on ideas rather than reject them.

Family Strategies that build cognitive flexibility

Ask: 'How many good solutions are there to this problem? What is the one you like best? Why?'

Every so often, you could play the Backwards Day Game. This helps kids break rigid thinking patterns and explore alternative actions. Pick a day (or part of a day) where things are done in reverse or in unexpected ways. For example:

- Eat dessert before dinner.
- Walk backwards to the car.
- Say 'Goodnight' in the morning and 'Good morning' at bedtime.
- Discuss: How did it feel to do things differently? What surprised you?

Two truths and an exception – in this activity we all think about a topic and say two things that are true – for example, 'Dogs bark and birds fly'. Then we try to find a way to make one or both of them not true – for example, 'Emus don't fly'.

Games that build cognitive flexibility

'What else could it be?' This is a drama game that builds cognitive flexibility. Take a common household object – a spoon, a pot, a vacuum cleaner – and ask how many other things this could be. For example, a spoon could be a paddle for a tiny boat or a bat for a sport played by very small people.

Games that have reversals of rules, such as Uno, or require quick thinking, such as charades, are also suitable.

Other suitable games include:

- chess
- backgammon
- checkers
- Fluxx
- computer games such as:
  - Minecraft
  - Civilisation VI
  - SimCity
  - Oxygen Not Included
  - RimWorld.

Chapter 19

Emotional Regulation

There are times when all of us need to calm ourselves down and there are times when we need to rev ourselves up. This is the skill of regulating our emotions.

If you have ever met someone who is unable to settle or calm themselves, who loses their temper, who misinterprets you and doesn't give you an opportunity to explain the misunderstanding, you will know how difficult it is to collaborate with them.

Being able to control and regulate your emotions is a powerful predictor of success in life. Without it, personal relationships become rollercoasters of high drama and work projects descend into mayhem. Emotional regulation makes it possible for other people to put up with you and work with you. If you can't manage yourself, it is difficult to manage anything else. This is why one of the key aims of parenting and teaching is to help neurodivergent kids who are emotionally dysregulated (out of sorts, upset, angry) to regain a sense of calm.

Helping your child develop emotional regulation

The body plays a more powerful role in calming the mind than the mind plays in calming the body. Most of the effective methods of calming or regulating the emotions of neurodivergent kids involve non-verbal soothing and physical exertion. The quickest way to calm the mind is to exert the body.

The SETTLE method for calming down

- **(S) Signals are useful.** Feelings like anxiety and upset tell us that we need to prepare for action. The physical symptoms of stress – being wired or hyper-alert, feeling agitated, breathing quickly, or feeling a bit buzzy and light-headed – all prepare us to either fight against something or run away from it. It is helpful to see your stress as a signal. Take four deep 'belly' breaths and breathe each one out s-l-o-w-l-y (silently counting out to yourself 'one thousand, two thousand, three thousand …').

- **(E) Embrace the fear.** Usually when we feel upset or angry we are fearing something. Ask yourself, 'What am I feeling fearful or scared about at the moment?' and 'Is this fearful situation really going to happen or am I just imagining the worst possible outcome?'

- **(T) Take it slow.** Even if you need to act immediately, it is best to prepare yourself to do so effectively. Rub behind each of your ears and sigh slowly, then gently rub the small hollow at the back of your neck in a circular fashion for 30 seconds. Hum to yourself.

- **(T) Take a walk.** It's time to use the energy that stress has given you. If you can, go for a walk or run, and while you are doing so, shift your eyes from side to side as you take in the environment.

- **(L) Lessen your time frame.** Try to sharpen your focus to what you can do now. Be here now.

- **(E) Express your coping statements.** These could include: 'I've got this' or 'I get to do this' or 'Anyone who ever did anything important felt some stress' or 'I wouldn't be doing this if it wasn't worthwhile.' Then complete the statement: 'Once I've done this, I can …' This builds positive anticipation.

Activities that build emotional regulation

- rev-ups and slowdowns – this involves doing things quickly and then doing something slowly (for example, 'Let's clean up this room as quickly as possible and then we'll go for ice cream')

- modelling good people skills to children – ask yourself out loud, 'Why am I feeling this way?' and show them it is ok to say, 'I am feeling ... at the moment. I need to do something different'
- masks and puppets depicting different feelings
- imagining what you want to happen
- colour-coding moods
- body-mapping emotions – draw your feelings and indicate where in your body you notice each feeling (for example, is anger in your stomach or chest or fists?)
- dance and movements that express feelings
- yoga, tai chi, aikido, and stretching
- calming spots, chill-out rooms
- music and headphones
- doodling, drawing, completing mazes
- going for a walk or run
- drinking water or splashing your face with cold water.

Family strategies that build emotional regulation

- stop, think, do – pause and reconsider
- differentiating between 'meltdowns' (out of control) and 'cool-downs' (retaining some control)
- learning the early-warning signals of upset and frustration in your child – tense jaw, louder voice, trembling, hands forming fists
- using physical signals to assist in calming – move somewhere else, shake it out, run it out, dance it out
- doing something else before trying to solve the upset.

Games that build emotional regulation

Games such as Slenderman, Flappy Bird, Tap the Frog, and Ant Smasher help kids to recognise their emotional reactions to different experiences.

Chapter 20
Your Next Steps to Unleashing Neuroadvantage

The moment you see your child's difference as a gift, you begin to change their future.

Parenting or teaching children teaches us a lot about who we are. We learn how we cope when we are at full capacity, how we manage when we are feeling so tired we can barely think, and how we respond to moments that daunt us or make us feel terrified. It is not for the faint-hearted.

Add neurodivergence to the mix and all that ratchets up several notches. Parenting or teaching neurodivergent kids stretches us in ways we could never anticipate. At each step we are recalibrating and refining our ways of helping. There are times when we feel overwhelmed.

As the steps towards success always have to be shaped to meet the needs, interests and learning strengths of each child, we need to learn and then re-learn the individuality of each child. There will be times when we will need to second-, third- and even fourth-guess ourselves as we rethink what approach will be effective.

This is necessarily energy- and time-consuming and requires us to be purposeful and intentional, but the payoff in terms of setting our kids up for great lives is enormous.

From struggles to strengths

You've reached the final chapter, but really this is the beginning of a much more powerful process. Because now you're not just reading about strengths-based parenting – you're ready to live it.

Over these pages, you've seen how neurodivergence doesn't mean brokenness. It means difference. It means opportunity. And when parents and teachers step forward with insight, belief and courage, everything begins to shift.

One of the major challenges for parents of neurodivergent kids when major decisions need to be made is only having access to one voice in their head – their own. The truth is, adding in a support team is essential to achieve your child's full potential and maximise results.

So where do you go from here?

I invite you to take these next five steps – not just for your child, but for your peace of mind, your confidence and your family's path forward.

Step 1: Consider recommending or even buying a copy of this book for your child's teacher

Maybe it's a teacher, a relative or another parent who feels overwhelmed or lost. Share this book and these ideas with them. When teachers and parents work together, the outcomes for children improve.

Creating optimal outcomes for neurodivergent kids is a treasure hunt. It requires support, nuance and a determination to keep trying strategies until the right approaches click into place.

For the person you share this with, it might be the beginning of their turning point too.

Step 2: Write your parent mission statement

This is your anchor. Your compass. Your declaration.

'I want to raise my child with courage, clarity and conviction. I believe their brain is beautiful, and I will help them discover their brilliance.'

At the end of this chapter, you'll find a space to write your Parent Mission Statement – your personal commitment to being the kind of guide your child needs.

Step 3: Discover your child's learning strengths

Take ten minutes to complete the learning strengths analysis at www.mylearningstrengths.com. It's completely free – and it might be one of the most affirming things you've ever done as a parent.

You'll have a clearer picture of how your child's brain works best – and how you can support that brilliance.

You might also consider completing your own learning strengths analysis.

Step 4: Get the full report

You've seen the surface – now dive deeper. The full learning strengths report gives you:

- Tailored strategies for learning and motivation
- Insights into how your child thinks, remembers, plans and thrives
- Tips for advocating at school and home.

It's not just information – it's a practical guide for action.

Step 5: Book a Zoom session with me

If you'd like expert guidance, I offer private 1:1 Zoom consultations for parents. These don't need to be very frequent, but they do give you access to a support person who can guide you towards the latest research and useful devices and help you make wise decisions to create a great future for your child.

We'll walk through your child's strengths profile, explore your current challenges, and build an action plan tailored to your child and family.

To book your session, visit https://andrewfuller.com.au/counselling/ or email me directly at inyahead@aussiebb.com.au.

This is not the end – it's the invitation

Parenting a neurodivergent child isn't about fixing them. It's about finding them – and fiercely supporting who they're becoming.

If this book has helped you see your child differently, then the real work – and the real joy – begins now.

Together, let's move from awareness to action. From fear to confidence. From struggle… to **neuroadvantage!**

Parenting Mission Statement – for You and Your Neurodivergent Child

1. What matters most to you?

1. What are the values you most want to live by as a parent?
2. What kind of parent do you aspire to be when things are calm? When things are stressful?
3. When you look back in ten years, what do you want your child to say they felt most from you?
4. Which of your beliefs about success, learning and behaviour might you need to re-examine?

2. Understanding your child's strengths and needs

Who is your child – really?

5. What are your child's natural learning strengths, talents or fascinations – even if they're not school-related?
6. In what settings or activities does your child come alive? When do they shut down?
7. What patterns have you noticed in how they think, feel and learn?
8. What needs does your child have that are frequently misunderstood by others (or even by you)?

3. Relationships and connection

How do you want your relationship to feel?

9. What kind of emotional connection do you want to build with your child?
10. Which behaviours or responses from you help that connection? Which ones hurt it?
11. How do you help your child feel safe, seen and supported – especially when they're struggling?
12. How do you want to respond to meltdowns, shutdowns or oppositional behaviour?

④ Caring for yourself

13. How much sleep do you need to function well in your life?
14. What routines can you put into your week to improve your wellbeing and your coping capacity?
15. What foods seem to result in better moods for you and for your child?
16. How much physical activity do you need to remain healthy?

⑤ Hopes, goals and long-term vision

Where are you heading together?

17. What do you hope your child will believe about themselves by the time they leave home?
18. What skills (not just academic) do you want to help them develop over the next five years?
19. What does success look like for *your* family – not just according to society or school?
20. How can you support your child to become their best self, not someone else's version of 'normal'?

Putting it together: The elevator pitch and mission statement formula

Now try to summarise and synthesise your thoughts into a simple memorable statement:

I aim to parent by

Because

And I hope that my child will

Try to write this down on a small piece of cardboard and keep it in your wallet or purse.

Appendices

What parents need to know before meeting school staff

All students have the right to quality learning experiences at school.

In Australia, schools' responsibilities to cater to the needs of neurodiverse students are outlined in:

- The Disability Discrimination Act 1992
- The Disability Standards for Education 2005.

These require schools to make reasonable adjustments to help neurodivergent students to take part in education on the same basis as other students.

Checklist for meeting with schools

- Will the school grounds be open at any stage so that I can guide my child around and show them the location of key rooms before the year starts?
- If not, can I please have a map of the school with these places marked out?
- Who can I contact if I feel concerned about my child's progress at school?
- Is there a peer or buddy system at the school?

Profile sheet for your child's teachers

Name of child (insert recent photo)	Age
	Date of birth

Address	
Contact person	Phone
Email	
Back-up person	Phone
Email	
Key professionals involved	
Name	Phone
Email	
Parental approval to contact given: ☐ Yes ☐ No	
Best strategy if child becomes distressed or overwhelmed	
Emergency plan (if needed)	
Needs and possible behaviours	
Interests	
Learning strengths	
Learning challenges	
Strategies or interventions that have been either recommended or used to overcome these challenges	

Author's Notes

Introduction
- Page 1: 'Without the help of these neurodivergent people, none of us would be here.' Eccles, J. C. (1989). *Evolution of the brain: Creation of the self.* Routledge. Williams, J., & Taylor, E. (2006). The evolution of hyperactivity, impulsivity and cognitive diversity. *Journal of the Royal Society, Interface, 3* (8), 299–413.
- Page 2: 'About 60 per cent of the neurodivergent brain is myelinated, which of course means about 40 per cent is not.' Buzsaki, G. (2019). *The brain from inside out.* Oxford University Press. Dehaene, S. (2014). *Consciousness and the brain: Deciphering how the brain codes our thoughts.* Viking Press. Sterling, P., & Laughlin, S. (2015). *Principles of neural design.* MIT Press.

Chapter 1
- Page 13: 'there are two main pathways in the brain.' Kosslyn, S. M., & Miller, G.W. (2015). *Top brain, bottom brain.* Simon and Schuster. Post, B. B. (2009). *The great behavior breakdown.* Post Publications.

Chapter 2
- Gros, D. F. (2021). *Overcoming avoidance.* New Harbinger.
- Page 26: 'Around 17 per cent of people suffer high levels of mathematics anxiety.' Boaler, J. (2016). *Mathematical mindsets.* Jossey-Bass. Butterworth, B. (2018). *Dyscalculia: From science to education.* Routledge.

Chapter 3
- Baron-Cohen, S. (2002). *The pattern seekers.* Penguin.

Chapter 4
- Badre, D. (2020). *On task: How our brain gets things done.* Princeton University Press.
- Greenblatt, J., & Gottlieb, B. (2017). *Finally focused.* Harmony Books.

- Guare, R., Guare, C., & Dawson, P. (2013). *Smart but scattered teens.* Guilford.
- Hartmann, T. (2019). *ADHD: A hunter in a farmer's world.* Healing Arts Press.
- Mark, G. (2023). *Attention span.* William Collins.

Chapter 6

- Post, B. B. (2009). *The great behavior breakdown.* Post Publications.

Chapter 7

- Bloomberg, H., with Dempsey, M. (2011). *Movements that heal: Rhythmic movement training and primitive reflex integration.* BookPal.
- Goddard Blythe, S. (2012). *Neuromotor immaturity in children and adults: The INPP screening test for clinicians and health practitioners.* John Wiley & Sons.
- Pack, B. (2019). *Brain activation incorporating vestibular and cardiovascular regimens.*
- Taylor, M., Houghton, S., & Chapman, E. (2004). Primitive reflexes and attention-deficit/hyperactivity disorder: Developmental origins of classroom dysfunction. *International Journal of Special Education, 19*(1), 23–37.

Chapter 8

- Chouake, T., Levy, T., Javitt, D. C., & Lavidor, M. (2012). Magnocellular training improves visual word recognition. *Frontiers in Human Neuroscience, 6.*
- Franklin, D. (2018). *Helping your child with language-based learning disabilities.* New Harbinger.
- Wolf, M. (2019). *Reader, come home: The reading brain in a digital world.* Harper Collins.

Chapter 9

- Butterworth, B. (2018). *Dyscalculia: From science to education.* Routledge.
- Clement, G. F. (2017). *Exploring the influence of the Singapore modeling method on prospective elementary teachers in a university mathematics course.* [Doctoral dissertation, Georgia State University.] https://scholarworks.gsu.edu/cgi/viewcontent.cgi?article=1035&context=ece_diss

- Day, L., & Lovitt, C. (2011). *Effectively teaching mathematics.* https://andrewfuller.com.au/wp-content/uploads/2014/08/Effectively-teaching-mathematics.pdf
- Dehaene, S. (2011). *The number sense: How the mind creates mathematics* (Rev. ed.). Oxford University Press.

Chapter 10

- Dehaene, S. (2010). *Reading in the brain: The new science of how we read.* Penguin.

Chapter 12

- Bellis, T. J. (2002). *When the brain can't hear.* Pocket Books.
- Tan, L. (1999). *Auditory processing at school.* Listening Works.

Part 2

- Dehaene, S. (2020). *How we learn.* Penguin
- Diamond. A. (2012). Activities and programs that improve children's executive functions. *Current Directions in Psychological Science, 21*(5), 335–41.
- Diamond, A. (2013). Executive functions. *Annual Review of Psychology, 64,* 135–68.
- Diamond, A., Barnett, S., Thomas, J., & Munro, S. (2007). Preschool program improves cognitive control. *Science, 318,* 1387–88.
- Diamond, A., & Lee, K. (2011). Interventions shown to aid executive function development in children 4–12 years old. *Science, 333*(6045), 959–64.
- Powell, M. (2023). *Executive functioning superpowers: Inclusive strategies that embrace neurodiversity at home and in the classroom.*

Acknowledgments

To all my clients who didn't realise they were also my teachers.

Many other people have kindly contributed to the development of these ideas – in particular:

- Lucy Thomas
- Juan Becher
- Andrew Campbell
- Alica Cohen
- Daniel Cohen
- Ian Fagan
- Julian Fagan
- Vicki Hartley
- Liz Keable

www.ingramcontent.com/pod-product-compliance
Lightning Source LLC
Chambersburg PA
CBHW011300070526
44584CB00027BA/3792